Skip

Coryell

White Feather Press

Making the world a better place - one reader at a time.

Laughter

and

Tears

Living Both Sides of Life

Other Books by Skip Coryell

Bond of Unseen Blood
Stalking Natalie
RKBA: Defending the Right to Keep and Bear Arms
We Hold These Truths
Blood in the Streets
Church and State

Available at www.whitefeatherpress.com.

Signed copies are available only at
www.skipcoryell.com

Cover design created by Ron Bell of AdVision Design Group
(www.advisiondesigngroup.com)

ISBN - 978-1-4537315-6-7

Printed in the United States of America

Dedicated to my wife,

Sara. Thank you.

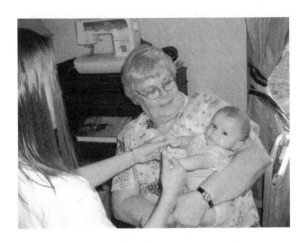

Many thanks to my mother. You have been a source of hope and inspiration.

Also, many thanks to the following for their input and support in writing this book:

Pastor Jeff Arnett

Dr. Dianne Portfleet

Dr. Hadley Kigar

Dave Maqueen

Pastor Timm Oyer

Introduction

Pain will always change you. It will make you better, or it will make you worse. The key to growing through that pain, is your positive response. It is your choice. You, alone, decide.

M. Scott Peck, in his now-famous book *"The Road Less Traveled"* made the following statement: "A wise man welcomes pain and sees it as a way to grow." During my first divorce, I clung to that saying, milking it for all it was worth, using it to help me grow as much as possible. But by the time my second divorce rolled around, I was so tired of pain, that I cried like a baby. I lashed out. I revolted. "No! I don't want to grow anymore! Please God, let me stay a fool!"

But God, our loving father, calmly stroked the furled brow of my heart and said, *"Relax child. Just relax. You don't have to be perfect. You just have to survive. Relax, and I will help you."*

And God did help me, but in the most unexpected way. God taught me how to laugh. While growing through my pain, I accumulated a smidgen of wisdom and perspective, and these two traits pointed me to joy and laughter - the other side of life.

Laughter and tears are the medicinal balm of life. They both heal, empower, and exhort, but they were created to be mutually inclusive. They are two sides of the same coin. To have one and not the other is to go through life with a lop-sided personality. All tears and you may end up hopelessly bitter and morose. Conversely, too much laughter, and you may dance through life, never growing wise, never grappling with the eternal questions of "Why".

Laughter and tears are beautiful gifts from God. Liken them to a pair of wonderful shoes. If you wear one, without the other, the best you can hope for is to limp along through life, doing less than what God intended for you.

But if you can merge the two, incorporate both of them appropriately into your life, then you will be freed to live life fully and to better serve others.

And now, I wish you the best, as you laugh and cry your way through God's gift of life.

Skip Coryell, 2007

Author's Note

I first wrote Laughter and Tears back in 2006. At that time I was living in Michigan with my wife and 3 kids. Today (in 2010) we have added another child and we have moved twice. Aside from my writing, I now work full time as President of White Feather Press. I enjoy publishing other authors almost as much as writing my own books. That surprised me.

I just wanted to thank you for reading my book. You can contact me anytime by going to www.skipcoryell.com.

God bless you and your family.

Skip Coryell, 2010

"It is by not always thinking of yourself, if you can manage it, that you might somehow be happy. Until you make room in your life for someone as important to you as yourself, you will always be searching and lost."

--Richard Bach--

"We live very close together. So, our prime purpose in this life is to help others. And if you can't help them, at least don't hurt them."

--The Dalai Lama--

Green Spiral Notebook

I remember the first journal entry I ever wrote. I was 16 years old. Mr. Resnik, my literature teacher, had assigned us the task, and I took to it like a fish to water. I had never written much before, but I found it cathartic and refreshing. I was a lonely youth, troubled, a bit withdrawn, and angry as well. I came from one of those "dysfunctional" families you're always hearing about, and my faith in God was waning to say the least. I struggled daily, trying to make sense of my troubled family, desperately attempting to figure out the meaning of life. "Why am I here?" That's the universal question isn't it? Why are we here? Where is the meaning? And, if there is no meaning, then what is the point? Why live at all?

The search for meaning in life is one of the things that distinguish us from the animals. A bear, a monkey, a rat; they live, they breed, they die, with no thought to the eternal question of "why". We humans put a high price tag on meaning. We value it; indeed, cannot live without it. We are creatures of purpose, created in the image of our God, always searching, always asking, the ever, eternal, "why".

Originally, this book began as a page on my website (www.skipcoryell.com) titled "Inside Skip's Brain". It was an on-line journal where I could write whatever I wanted. The first page contained the following caution:

"Welcome to the inside of my brain. It's a scary place in here, because you never know what I'm going to think. But be strong and brave, and you should make it out alive.

This link will be updated weekly with, you guessed it, whatever is on my mind at the time. Sometimes it will be funny, sometimes serious, sometimes downright stupid and outrageous. At any rate, I hope you enjoy your stay inside my brain. Don't forget to clean up before you leave."

Surprisingly enough, *"Inside Skip's Brain"* quickly became the most popular page on my website, with many people returning over and over again to read the weekly entries. I kept asking myself: Why do people like it so much? Because I honestly didn't understand. They told me that they could relate to what I was saying on an emotional and spiritual level. When they read my stories, they felt like they were reading about themselves. I guess in a way, they were.

Journaling is an important tool for self-discovery, and here is what I found out about myself: "God and family are the two most important aspects of my life. The two are inseparable; they weave together seamlessly, like the purple robe of Christ, cut from the same cloth, woven together as one, and were never intended to be rent.

King Solomon said in the book of Ecclesiastes, "There is nothing new under the sun." I suppose that refers to thoughts as well as to actions. So that means that anything I can think of, someone before me has already pondered, perhaps hundreds of years ago, or maybe even today. I believe that all people, regardless of race, or time, or condition, have much in common. We were all created in God's image, so that makes us all basically the same. We all wonder about God. We all care about family.

So it should come as no surprise that my thoughts are your thoughts, and that they are, in some way, universal to mankind. At any rate, faith and family are important to everyone, even to those who pretend it's not.

In one of my first journal entries, at the impressionable and searching age of 16, I wrote down the following entry in my diary:

"Sometimes I wonder why we're here? How did we get here? Is it like in the Bible? Did God create us? Or is it something else? Maybe we're just part of someone else's dream? He could wake up, and that would be the end of us all."

At 16 years of age, I didn't know a whole lot about life, but I have always been a searching being. I think most people are. We all ask the higher questions, perhaps not out loud, but in the stillness, in the darkness of our hearts, we can't help but ask: "Why am I here?"

That first, green, spiral notebook was the beginning of a lifelong journey, because the act of writing down my thoughts and innermost feelings changed my life forever. After that, I never stopped writing – I never looked back. Thirty-two years later, I still have those notebooks, old, faded, torn and stained. Sometimes I open them up, read, and laugh. At other times, I read and cry.

But my point is this: None of us were able to map out our lives like a bus schedule. We can plan and scheme with the best and worst of intentions, but despite that, one thing rings clear: God is in control, and He has ideas of His own. True, He lets us make our own decisions (for good or ill) but in the end, He has a way of getting what He wants. I like God. He's a good old boy. He's the best Daddy in the world.

I'm relieved that I never knew how my life would turn out, that I would marry three times and divorce twice, that a multitude of pain would be visited upon me, assailing me from many angles. I suppose it's true: sometimes ignorance is bliss. And I'm happy for my mistakes as well as my good choices. There is no future in regret.

"Love and respect are the most important aspects of parenting, and of all relationships."

--Jodie Foster--

I always had mixed feelings on the way
home, because leaving two kids in Georgia, also brought me closer to my youngest
two, Cathy and Phillip, in Michigan. I think
that must be what children feel when they
are shuffled from one parent's home to the
other.

Crying on a Georgia Mountainside

Today I was cleaning out my files at work. I've collected a lot of "stuff" the past 20 years. Most of it I threw away, but there are two items I kept.

One is a dried-up Catalpa Bean, with dead Maple leaves tied to it by their stems. It doesn't look like much, but it means a great deal to me. My daughter, Cathy, then about 8 years old, had made it for me while sitting beside me at work. I was a single parent at the time and had gotten physical custody of her and my son, Phillip. I could never bring myself to throw that one away.

The second artifact is a sprig of Mountain Laurel I collected near the border of Georgia and Tennessee almost 10 years ago. I've been carting it around with me, giving it a place of honor on top of my computer screen here at work all this time. The leaves tell a story.

When my son, Chris, was around 10 years old, and my daughter, Marissa, was about 7, my first ex-wife moved away to Georgia and took my kids with her. That act crushed me for years to come. Because of that, I missed out on much of their childhood. It took me years to forgive her for that, and sometimes I still struggle with it.

I collected the Mountain Laurel on one of my trips down to visit them. I drove 14 hours down, saw them for about 6 hours, then had to drive straight back, going two days without sleep. That was the only way I could see Chris and Marissa. I would always drive quickly through the mountains on the way down, anxious to see them, knowing that every mile I drove was bringing me closer to them. On the way back, I would cry from Georgia all the way up through Tennessee and Kentucky, finally drying up by Ohio. But one time I stopped on a mountainside and climbed all the way up to the top. I could almost see my children's hometown from there, and it was very beautiful. On the way down the mountain, I took a sprig of Laurel in an effort to hold on to them and the moment.

But no memento can ever give me back the things that I missed. I will never reclaim that lost childhood times two. I always had mixed feelings on the way home, because leaving two kids in Georgia, also brought me closer to my youngest two, Cathy and Phillip, in Michigan. I think that must be what children feel when they are shuffled from one parent's home to the other. The world can be a sad state of affairs. But, if you want fair, play Monopoly.

My first published novel "*Bond of Unseen Blood*" was an expression of this loss. It was a cathartic attempt to memorialize all the times I wanted to take them to the park, but could not - all the times I wanted to go to their soccer games, but could not. Separation from my kids is, without a doubt, the most painful experience I've ever gone through.

If you haven't yet married, choose wisely. Some mistakes are easily forgiven and carry little consequence. But marrying the wrong person can set off a chain of pain that lasts for generations. Be careful.

All of us live or die based on the decisions we make. Be patient and make good decisions.

Baby Farts and Soccer Moms

I'm sitting in my old , dirty, beat-up pick up truck, in the parking lot of Goodwill Industries in Hastings, MI. I have a blanket over my head to keep out the light, so I can see my computer screen. My wife is nursing our 2-month old son, Cedar, and he just burped. Nice ambience. I love it, and can think of nowhere else I'd rather be. It's only a matter of time until I'm noticed by the police, and they stop to check things out. For all they know, I could be cooking meth under this blanket.

Now that would be an interesting situation, wouldn't it?

"Good morning officer. I'm writing a book; my baby is farting, and my wife is being milked to within an inch of her life. What seems to be the problem?"

"Driver's license, proof of insurance and registration please."

Have you ever noticed how polite police officers are? It doesn't matter how rude you are or what you say to them. They just always seem to stay calm and professional. I suppose I can identify with that aspect of their character. I've been a high school and college soccer official for 15 years now, and I can appreciate emotional restraint in the face of confrontation.

I've often wondered: What is it about sports that drives people so crazy? It's like we become were wolves, and sporting events are the equivalent of a full moon at midnight. Boy, could I tell you some stories. Hey! I'm a writer. I can do that. Let me tell you a story.

I think the worst game I ever refereed was about 10 years ago in a conservative and peaceful little town just south of Grand Rapids. It should have been an easy game, since the players were only 8 years old, but I'll remember that day forever.

The players were doing just fine. After all, what could they possibly do wrong? They were just little waifs, running around, having fun, trying to kick a white ball through two upright sticks. Sounds like fun. Right? Maybe.

How many of you have called the referee, "blind as a bat" or a "moron", an "idiot", or even something worse that I won't describe here. I believe I've been called every colorful expletive in the book. I think most of you have abused a referee at one point in your lives. I know I have.

But let's get back to my story. These were the parents from soccer-mom hell! They weren't just insulting me, they were crowding onto the field, swearing, even delivering obscene gestures. Eventually, I had to eject both coaches and end the game early. I hated to do it, because the kids wanted to play soccer, but I just couldn't allow the parents and coaches to act that way in front of their sons and daughters. I am a firm believer that "What you allow – you teach."

So after the game, I quickly walked away, only to have a crowd of otherwise respectable, middle-aged mothers follow me to the parking lot, screaming obscenities at the top of their voices, with 8-year olds in tow. I finally made it to my car and drove away without running over anyone.

But the saddest part of that day, even after 10 years of time to dull the pain, was the look of sadness and confusion on the faces of those children. They didn't understand what had happened to their parents. Why is mommy acting like Hitler on Quaaludes? Why is daddy threatening to shove the referee's whistle up into his rectum? It doesn't make sense. It is just a game – isn't it?

Maybe.

I recall another game several years ago, a boy's high school game, where the spectators were particularly vocal.

The game was going along fine despite the parents. The players were following the rules, and trying not to foul each other. Then, all of a sudden, one boy stopped dribbling the ball right in the middle of play and just stood there. All the other players stopped too. The boy looked over at me and asked in an exasperated voice. "Sir, will you please make the parents stop insulting us?"

I was amazed. This teenage boy got it. He understood, and he had the character and courage to stand up for himself. I nodded my head and said, "Sure. I can do that."

I jogged over to the bleachers and climbed the steps about halfway until I was in the middle of about 100 parents. I stopped and said.

"Now you people listen to me. You're not here to insult the players. You're not here to belittle the referee. You're here to encourage your kids and to cheer for them. You all should be ashamed of yourselves for acting this way. Your job is to teach your kids good sportsmanship, and if you can't do that, then I'll clear the stadium and we'll play without you."

Right about then, a very large man stood up and glared at me. It was an obvious testosterone challenge. I looked over at him and met his gaze. I pointed my finger at him as I spoke.

"And you sir, will be the first to go!"

He sat back down.

I jogged back down onto the field, blew my whistle, and the game continued. But the fans were unusually quiet for the rest of the match.

Our society, civilization in general, is all artificial; it's a thin veneer of politeness that can vanish in an instant.

The only difference between America and a third-world country, is the rule of law. And when the rule of law breaks down, so will America. Then things will revert to their natural state: the law of the jungle. Society is like a garden. Kill the weeds, or they will kill you.

I sometimes wonder what happened to that one boy who stood up and demanded that people respect him. And I wonder what happened to those 8 year olds who listened as their mothers and fathers cussed out the referee.

Isn't it amazing what people will do under cover of the crowd? The nicest soccer mom, the most loving father, is able to shed that thin veneer of courtesy, and go back 5,000 years to a time when the law of the jungle reigned supreme, when tooth, fang and claw was the only law.

Well, my wife is done nursing now. I look over and see her smiling face, the relaxed, sleeping form of my baby in her arms, enjoying the fruits of a civilized society. I want that thin veneer of civility to remain intact for the sake of my children and my grandchildren. I know you do too.

And always remember: What you allow – you teach. So teach good things. Your children are watching.

"Marriage and the up-bringing of children in the home require as well-trained a mind and as well-disciplined a character as any other occupation that might be considered a career."

--Eleanor Roosevelt--

My kids, Cathy and Phillip; they are energy incarnate. They always wanted to play, but some days it just wasn't in me. I would just lay on the couch and they would play games like, "Doctor Daddy", "Daddy's art class" and "Daddy's Beauty Parlor".

Daddy's Art Class

It's a snow day! We got dumped with 10 inches last night and my 9 and 11-year old are hanging all over me. I tickle them and wrestle until I'm too tired, then I go back to work at the computer.

My daughter is putting my hair in pony tails right now. Is it supposed to hurt this much? In years gone by, my son used to spread peanut butter on my bare back as I slept. That felt even worse.

I remember several years ago. I was a single parent, working three jobs, all four kids living with me. My day would end late and I'd collapse on the couch, totally exhausted. Of course the two little ones always wanted to play, but some days it just wasn't in me. I would just lay on the couch and they would play games like, "Doctor Daddy", "Daddy's art class" and "Daddy's Beauty Parlor". Sometimes I ended up passed out on the couch, with my then 8-year-old daughter, sitting on my chest, giving me a complete makeover. Does makeup always feel that yucky? Sometimes I went to the office feeling pretty … well, pretty – "pretty" I guess. I got a few stares, because that makeup doesn't always wash off like it's supposed to.

I remember one day in particular. I went into work the day after both my little ones had played "Daddy's Art Class". My co-workers stared at me funny every time I talked to someone. I thought for sure I'd gotten all the paint off my face. Finally, I went into the bathroom and looked in the mirror. Everything looked fine – until I blinked one eye. My son had painted one eyelid green, and the other bright orange.

It's so nice that children have a sense of humor and they teach us to laugh at ourselves.

We should never forget that. Life tends to be hard and full of pain, so we should never miss an opportunity to laugh at our mistakes. My children help me laugh and keep me whole and sane.

My children are the inspiration for some of the scenes I write in my novels.

Chapter 26 and 31 from "*We Hold These Truths*" were inspired by my kids. We used to play the "Lava Game" all the time until they got too big and kept hurting me. Here's an excerpt from Chapter 31 of "We Hold These Truths". If you love kids, you may enjoy it.

"Nurse, has the anastasia taken effect yet?"

Phillip was dressed in one of his father's baggy white dress shirts, and it hung down to his knees. There was a white dish towel wrapped and duct-taped to his head, and he was the perfect picture of a budding young surgeon.

"Let me check Doctor Philly."

Susan was dressed in similar garb, with a toy stethoscope around her neck, and a bowl full of kitchen utensils in her right hand. She walked around her four-year old brother, Micah, who was staring up Hank's nose from only 6 inches away.

"He sure gots a lot of hair up there."

Hank started to snore, and Micah moved back a few inches.

"What's he doin' Phillip?"

Phillip gave him an annoyed stare.

"He's snoring. I told you to call me Dr. Phil!"

Micah moved closer to the sound again and tried to look further up his father's nostrils.

"Can't we make it stop?"

Phillip's voice took on a confident, superior tone.

"Of course we can. I'm a doctor! I'll simply remove his snoring gland up there inside his naval cavity. But first we've got to take out his guts, cuz they're all inflected."

Cathy was wearing her favorite pink pajamas and laying on the back of the couch looking down on her father's sleeping body. She always liked it when he held still for them.

"Is it going to hurt, Doctor Phil?"

Phillip dug through the kitchen utensils and pulled out an egg beater and held it up to the light as if to inspect it.

"Only if he wakes up, Nurse Cathy."

Susan was bending over his face now and prying open his eyelids. She looked deep into Hank's bloodshot orbs.

"I think he's dead!"

"Don't be stupid, Nurse Susan! Dead people don't snore!"

She let her father's eyelids slam back shut and walked back to take her place beside the doctor. Phillip put the egg beater back in the bowl.

"Nurse, I'm ready to make the indecision."

He held out his right hand.

"Scalpel!"

A serious look came over Susan's face.

"Be careful Doctor. He's the only daddy we got."

Hank's flannel shirt was pulled up to his armpits, and Micah, whose attention to Hank's nose hair had been temporarily interrupted, was now drawing pictures on Hank's chest with colorful felt markers.

Cathy propped her head up on her elbow and looked on with interest while Phillip took the grey rubber hunting knife and began the imaginary cut across Hank's stomach. First, he cut out all the "inflection", then, one by one, each of Hank's organs were removed and handed to Nurse Susan who pretended to place them delicately in a 5-gallon bucket behind them.

"What do we do with all these parts when we're done Doctor Phil?"

Phillip looked up long enough to answer her, and as

he did, Susan swabbed imaginary sweat from his brow with a dirty dish rag.

First, we take 'em to the lab and look at 'em under a telescope. Then we give 'em to the pigs. Freida says pigs will eat anything."

Susan nodded her head knowingly.

"I guess he don't need 'em anymore anyways."

No one saw Micah reach over and take the small metal spoon out of the plastic bowl.

"All we got left is the ruptured tumor, and then we can do the circumspection."

Phillip handed the rubber knife back to Nurse Susan, who took it and quickly swabbed his forehead.

Suddenly, Hank awoke with a piercing scream and jumped up off the couch, all the while holding onto the spoon shoved deep inside his nose. Cathy fell off the back of the couch, and Micah, who had been straddling his father's chest was thrown completely clear.

"What are you guys doing!"

Hank pulled his hand away from his face and Phillip could barely see the end of the spoon through all the blood coming from the patient's nose. But the 10-year old doctor maintained his composure.

"Nurse! More anastasia!"

Hank fell down to the carpet, tugging at the end of the spoon, but it was firmly fixed to his snoring gland and wouldn't budge.

Nurse Susan ran screaming to her room and hid under

the bed while Cathy peeked out from behind the couch, and little Micah looked on with joy at all the excitement caused by his handiwork. Angela, who had been washing the dishes in the kitchen, heard the screaming and ran in dripping dishwater with every step.

Phillip alone remained calm.

"Sir, I think we're going to have to operate."

> "I felt as if I were walking with destiny, and that all my past life had been but a preparation for this hour and this trial."
>
> --Winston Churchill--

Destiny

I have never shared this with anyone before, either verbally or in written form, but I have always felt an overwhelming sense of destiny. Yes, I realize that statement smacks of self importance and perhaps even arrogance, but that's the only way I know how to say it. And as if that's not pompous enough, let me go even further by saying "I've always believed I would do something great in my life." I just didn't know what that great thing was. When I was younger, I always thought I would be a great writer. I believed that by age 30 I would win the Pulitzer Prize, and, later on in life, the Nobel Prize. However, by age 35 I was divorced, destitute, and still unpublished. At that point, I began to grow a little concerned. I suppose that's an understatement, because I was more than a little concerned: I was distraught. Not only was I not yet great, I was construed by some, including myself, as a total failure. So much for my legacy.

In an attempt to salve my distress, I began to refer

to myself as "the most pre-famous author you'll ever meet." Well, that was 14 years ago, and I'm still very pre-famous. And that's an optimistic statement. But there's one big difference: it just doesn't bother me so much anymore. It's not that I've lowered my goals or standards, it's just that I've come to realize that every person is destined to greatness. God has predestined it from the foundation of the world. He has planted a tiny seed of destiny inside each of us, and it is up to us to nurture and grow into all He has intended for us.

But there are many forces at work out there that will do their best to kill that seed and stunt its growth. I recall the words of my own father when I was 16 years old. I had done something wrong, gotten a bad grade in school I believe, and he was lecturing me. My father, though I love him, never really figured out the parenting thing and he often said or did things which were totally inappropriate or out of line. My father said to me, and I will remember these words my entire life: "Son, I don't care if you're a prostitute. Just be the best damned prostitute in the world!"

I remember being surprised, hurt, and confused all at the same time. Even as a child, I instinctively knew that his words were bizarre, but I just didn't know how to process it. I thought to myself, "I must be pretty worthless or he wouldn't say that about me." So I internalized, let it sink in and become a part of me. Here is what I heard him tell me: "Son, you're really not going to amount to much of anything in your life. I just hope you don't screw up too badly."

It reminds me of something I saw on the Jeff Foxworthy Show. Jeff was talking about his own backward, redneck family and he said, "I could walk upright and feed myself. In my family, that made me the pick of the litter!"

At the time, I was writing a journal for my English class in high school. I wrote the incident down, and I still have the journal somewhere. My English teacher read that and wrote in the margin. "You're kidding. He really said that?" In retrospect, I wish my teacher had taken me off to the side and explained to me that I really was a worthwhile person. I think it would have made a world of difference in how I turned out. But back then, teachers didn't meddle in "family affairs".

Now, as an adult, I realize that what my father said had nothing to do with me at all; it was more a statement about him than me. I wish I had known that. I wish someone had counteracted his damage. But a father is so important, is it even possible to repair a word-riddled son? I don't know. It has taken me decades to come this far on my own.

But what I've learned from it is this. A person's greatness has nothing to do with his career, his job, or his vocation. Greatness is defined by service to your fellow man. For me, I define my greatness by how I treat my wife and children.

Many times I find myself thinking, "I don't want to be like my father." That is the wrong approach. When I drive down the road, thinking to myself, don't go in the ditch; then I am focusing on the very thing I wish to avoid. Inevitably, I run off the road. The Bible says "When you put your hand to the plow, don't look back." That is good advice. Don't focus on what you don't want to become. Instead, keep your eyes on the prize, whether it's the Pulitzer, the Nobel, or better yet, being a great parent. Humility plus service equals greatness times two. It's a formula for destiny that you can live with.

The next time someone insults you, examine their words for validity. Ask yourself "Is it a statement about me or statement about them?" If it's you, then change. If it's not, then let it roll off you like water on a duck's back. Yes, I know. It's easier said than done. But do it anyways. You won't regret it.

"The purpose of human life is to serve and to show compassion and the will to help others."

--Albert Schweitzer--

Don't Make Me Wear a Tie

Today my co-workers are giving me a farewell luncheon. I've been at this company for over 20 years now, and this morning, as I reflect, I can't help but wonder: "How did I survive?" It's no secret that I'm no corporate pillar. I never dressed in the proper attire. I never talked the way the others did. I never really sang the corporate song or danced the company jig. I was a nonconformer.

So the question remains: "How did I survive for so long?"

I think it's a combination of a lot of things, but first and foremost, it's a tribute to my family. I had to provide for them, so I stuck it out. I've learned that doing the right thing, isn't always doing the easy thing.

Secondly, it's a tribute to the people I worked with. My boss was patient. In fact, I suspect that God may have sent me there just to teach him patience and tolerance. Although, when I'd walk in 15 minutes late, unshaven, wearing tennis shoes, flannel and camo; he may have argued against that point. But, he didn't fire me, and for that I thank him.

My co-workers were a strong and hardy lot, and they were kind enough to put up with me. Some people often wonder what others "really" think about them. Tom Sawyer comes to mind as I recall with a smile how he attended his own funeral and relished at the eulogy. Many days I would wander the rigid, professional, world of "the Company", in a daze, and pray: "Dear God, please don't make me wear a tie." I'm still trying to figure out how they could see me through all the camouflage I was wearing. I never really wanted to be noticed, and I always wondered, "What do they "really" think of me?"

I learned a lot of things in the corporate world: graphs and charts, mergers and downsizing, bottom lines, capital equipment, and private ventures. And now, after 20 years, I can finally admit: "I never really understood much of what they were paying me to do." A wise person once told me: "Just keep faking it until it's real." Well, I kept faking it, but it never did get real for me.

One of my favorite movies about the corporate world is called "*Office Space*". In it, Jennifer Anniston plays Joanna, the girlfriend to Peter Gibbons, a Software Engineer, who is unhappy with his job. Joanna is a waitress and also hates her employment. In a desperate attempt to escape the corporate "cubicle" world, Peter orchestrates a computer scam to rip off the company, but gets caught. In the end, Joanna gives him some good advice about life.

Peter says: "I don't know why I can't just go to work and be happy like I'm supposed to like everyone else."

Joanna: "Peter, most people don't like their jobs, but you go out there and you find something that makes you happy."

Peter: "I may never be happy at my job, but I think that if I could be with you, that I could be happy with my life."

Like Peter, I was never happy with the corporate lifestyle; it just didn't fit me, but I did it for my family, and I found other meaning outside of work. Now, as I write, I can't help but smile, because now I'm happy with my life and with my job.

Probably the most important thing I learned from the corporate world, was the importance of doing the job for which you were created. I knew from the start that God had other plans for me. I hated the corporate lifestyle, and wanted to leave everyday of my life. I knew God wanted me to write. But try as I may, I always seemed trapped inside the corporation, either by financial realities, or by the natural consequences of my own mistakes.

It was true. God had plans for me from the start, but first he had to prepare my heart and my soul to do the job. The corporate world, though not my calling, was one of the experiences of my life that God used to prepare me for my service to God and man. Moses spent 40 years herding sheep in the desert of Midian. It was not his life's calling, but he was faithful to it and he did the best job he could. Then God called him away, and Moses reluctantly obeyed. Now he was ready to do the work of his life.

Now, I am ready to write, ready to do whatever God tells me.

So, today, no longer faking it, I bid farewell to the corporate world. Thanks for tolerating me as long as you did. I'll never have to fake it again.

Phillip and Cedar love to play video games.
Phillip has been through a lot, but despite that
he's come through the fire like shining brass!
He's very proud of his baby brother, and he
works hard to be the best example he can be.

"In the little world in which children have
their existence, whosoever brings them up,
there is nothing so finely perceived and so
finely felt as injustice."

--Charles Dickens--

Eating Dirty Pizza

It's early in the morning, my wife is off to work,
and I'm sitting here in the recliner, watching my 9-year
old son, Phillip, play with his baby brother on the blanket. Phillip has been through a lot, more than any boy
should have to endure. Divorce takes a terrible toll on
the young.

Phillip was forced to watch his mother and father's
marriage break apart. That must have been very painful
for him. He had to sit idly by and watch as his mother
tried to drink herself to death. He had to watch, as she
jumped from one man's bed to another, and another, and
another.

And then he had to watch, helplessly, as she con-
tracted cancer. He watched, month, by month, by month,
as his mother, the one he loved, wasted away and finally
died. The little boy was then 7 years old, and he never really understood. I can safely surmise that, because I was
46 and I didn't understand it either. She was too young to

die. But then, isn't everyone?

I went to Oak Hill cemetery yesterday in the town where I was born and raised to see my father. It has been over 20 years since he died, and I still think of him everyday. I'm confused by that, because he wasn't really a very good father. But I still love him, and I miss him. Fathers have a profound impact on their children. Fatherhood is a picture of God, but He is the only perfect father. Unfortunately, He is spirit, and I am flesh. I used to hate that and cry in my lonely, dark times, because God could not hold me and make me feel better. Sometimes I would get angry at God for not meeting that need, but, later in life, I came to realize that it wasn't God who was supposed to meet that need; it was my father here on earth, and he wasn't doing it.

Now, as a father myself, I work hard to meet those needs which God the Spirit father has delegated to me, the physical, earthly father. I shower my children with affection. They need it. All children do. That's why God gave us mothers and fathers, to make sure those needs are met. But adults, like children, don't always do as they're told and sometimes children suffer for it.

We were looking at the gravestones yesterday. They come in so many different shapes, sizes, materials, and markings. My 11-year old daughter was commenting on them. It is so easy to talk about death when your whole life is still ahead of you. But something happens later on. We age. At about 30, our bodies begin to die, cells no longer regenerate as they once did, hair falls out, skin dries and wrinkles, and joints wear out and bring us pain. Our bodies, which once brought us pleasure, eventually become prisons of torture and pain, helping us to realize that soon we will die.

As a child, I used to wonder why God didn't let us live forever here on earth in our physical bodies, but now I think I understand it better. God created us with free will – the capacity to choose between doing good, or doing evil. Imagine the carnage that someone like Joseph Stalin and Adolf Hitler could have done as immortals. Much of life's deterrence and pending accountability would be gone. No fear of death, no judgment for past wrongs, no consequences. They could do anything they wanted, for as long as they wanted. Between those two men alone, they tortured and killed tens of millions of people.

Thank you God for physical mortality.

But this physical life is just the beginning, just the testing grounds for all of eternity. I have a feeling, that how we live in this life, helps determine how we live in the next.

Halfway through writing this, my son came up and asked me to play with him. I didn't want to. Inside I rattled off all the reasons I had to tell him no. I wanted to deny his request. I wanted him to go away. But there are limits to my own hypocrisy and selfishness, and this time I said yes.

I played with my son, and God rejoiced in heaven. After all, he's only 9, and he's already been through more than any boy should have to endure. Yes, there is a time for pain, but there is also a time to heal. I want the best for my son, the same way my father in heaven wants the best for me.

I just looked into the kitchen and saw my son getting into the pizza without asking. As I watched, he dropped some pepperoni onto the floor. He reached down and picked it up, brushed it off on his shirt, then glanced around to make sure no one was watching before popping it into his mouth. I suppose I should yell at him, but something inside just won't let me.

After all, it's not really all that important – just a little bit of dirty pizza.

"As the family goes, so goes the nation and so goes the whole world in which we live."
                                    --Pope John Paul II--

My oldest daughter is now 18. Marissa and I would hunt for morel mushrooms every Spring. She thought I could smell them.

A Fungus Among Us

I slowly stood up in front of 50 other people, in a room quiet enough to hear a horsefly chewing his cud. I nervously clasped my hands together and squeezed my fingers until the knuckles turned white. When I finally spoke, I could feel the shakiness in my voice. "Hello, my name is Skip Coryell, and I'm a fungaholic."

"There, I said it! Yes! I'm a mycophagist! I eat fungus, and I'm proud of it!"

Suddenly a weight lifted from my shoulders, and I felt the shame I'd known since childhood peeling off my back like the dead skin on a molting rattlesnake. But once I had started my confession, I couldn't stop. I ranted on and on, the cathartic raving taking on a life of its own. I had been forewarned that once you start down the dark, fungal path, forever will it dominate your destiny. But I hadn't listened. Like so many people before me, I thought I could handle my fungi.

"Okay, I admit it! I eat fungus. I eat it alone! I eat it

with friends! I even eat it early in the day when no one is looking! And once I take that first bite - I just can't stop until every mushroom in sight is slowly being digested inside me, becoming one with my alimentary canal. I can't help it! Fungi is fun!"

Okay, so now you must be thinking, "He's lost it. What kind of mushroom is he eating? Must be those hallucinogenic kind that grow in the desert."

No, I just like to eat Morel mushrooms, that's all. I've been eating morels since I was a kid, since I was old enough to walk. My mother and father introduced me to the past-time and I've been hooked ever since. If you grew up in the Midwest or in the Pacific Northwest, you probably know what I'm talking about, since they are very prevalent there. They come out in the Spring, usually in the month of May, and the season lasts but for a few weeks.

They are served as a delicacy in fancy restaurants and redneck homes alike, the main difference being the price. (Us rednecks don't eat anything unless we gather or kill it ourselves.) That reminds me of the first time I was ever in a fancy restaurant. I was just a simple country boy at the time, fresh off the farm, and I knew very little on how "the other half" lived.

The restaurant specialized in seafood, but, since I didn't know a crab from a crawdad, I let my experienced lady friend order for me. She started out with a glass of fine wine. I can't remember what they called it. I asked for Mountain Dew. Then she ordered a Shrimp Cocktail. I thought it was a fancy mixed drink, but when it came, it appeared to be just a big plate of shrimp with some red sauce in the middle. I was starving, so I dug in right away.

I was surprised when I picked up the first shrimp. It wasn't what I had expected. Wanting to impress my date, I called the waiter over and scolded him.

"Sir, these shrimp are cold! Now take them back to the kitchen and try again!"

My lady friend burst out laughing along with everyone in earshot. Fortunately, she thought I was joking, so I seized the moment and laughed along with her.

That was a long time ago, but I've avoided fancy restaurants since that day. They make me feel uncomfortable. But then, I digress.

Morel hunting has always been synonymous with family for me, and it's been a rock-steady constant for me my whole life. I can remember walking slowly through the woods beside my father, trying to stay behind him so he wouldn't yell at me when I stepped on one of them. In my younger years, I got yelled at a lot, and I swore I would never do that to my children. I lied.

But one thing is for certain, my kids and I have enjoyed hunting for morels every Spring. Fungus is a family thing at our home. Yesterday, we all went out to the woods, and we initiated young 2-month old Cedar into the fungal family fold. I'm not sure he understood the importance of the outing, but it's something we'll remember forever. My back is still sore from carrying him up and down hills for three hours. We found about 5 pounds of mushrooms and we're having a fish and mushroom fry at my brother's house this weekend. You see, once again, it's a family thing. Fungus is family.

I guess what I'm trying to get at is this: all families need tradition; they need fun; they need to do things together that the kids will remember long after they've grown up and moved away. Preferably, it will be something they enjoyed enough to pass on to their children as well. If the kids don't like it, then they won't pass it on. That's why I always go out of my way to show them a good time.

I always noticed that small children get bored when they don't find mushrooms, so I would often help them out. I convinced my children that I could smell the mushrooms when they got close, and then I would guide them to the right spot.

"I smell one over there."

Then I would point with my finger to the ground about 15 feet in front of me.

"Where Dad? I can't see it."

"Straight ahead of me about 15 feet."

They would move closer.

"Careful. It smells very close to me now."

A serious look would come over them.

"Where do you smell it now?"

"I smell it about 2 feet from your left shoe."

"Hey! I found it!"

Isn't it amazing what lies children will believe?

We should be careful what we tell them. My 9 and 11 year old have just figured out that I can't really find mushrooms by smell. I was afraid they would be upset with my lie, but they weren't. It brought them loads of fun, and they enjoyed it. They don't believe in Santa Claus or the tooth fairy anymore either. Instead, they believe in me.

But it was fun for a while, and it's something they tell to all their friends at school. I suppose the only thing profound about fungus is the joy it brings to my family. I recommend that all families find something they enjoy together and then do it often. Because, it's not about fungus, or sleeping outside in tents, or traveling across the country for 12 hours in a cramped car - it's about building memories; it's about bonding; it's about being together.

Find something your kids enjoy, and do it with them. They grow up too fast and the window of opportunity passes quickly. I regret that I was unable to spend more time with my two older children, and I wish I could change that. But you can't go back in time, and those moments I didn't spend with them are like a vacuum in my heart, always aching to be filled, but never will be.

Cathy and Phillip with their mother. The last six months of her life she was the best mother she had ever been. She met God on good terms.

Bull Named Fu Man Chu

This morning, on my way to dropping the kids off to school, I was listening to B-93, and one of my favorite songs (by Tim McGraw) came on. It goes like this:

"I was in my early forties,
With a lot of life before me,
An' a moment came that stopped me on a dime.
I spent most of the next days,
Looking at the x-rays,
An' talking 'bout the options an' talkin' 'bout sweet time."
I asked him when it sank in,
That this might really be the real end?
How's it hit you when you get that kind of news?
Man whatcha do?"

It reminded me of a day, almost two years ago, when my former-wife, Diana, called to tell me she had Ovarian Cancer. I was shocked and horrified. My first thought was for my children. How would I tell them that their mother was dying? My second thought was for her, because I knew she had led a very confused life, and that she wasn't ready to die.

I ran across this old journal entry, so I've included it below. It tells the story better than I can recall it.

11 February 2004

Two days ago from this writing, I received a call from Diana, and she told me that she had just been diagnosed with Ovarian cancer and that it appeared to be in the advanced stages of the disease. Her ovaries are enlarged and swollen; her lymph nodes are enflamed; and her body cavity is filling up with a fluid called acites. She was crying uncontrollably, and was very open to what I had to say to her. Something inside told me that she would die soon, that she would not recover from this illness. My first thoughts were for my children. I didn't want to tell them that their mother was dying of cancer. My second thoughts were to Diana. I knew she was not ready to die. I knew that she had to prepare herself to meet God.

I was very frank with her, and this is what I told her.

"Diana, the most important thing right now, whether you die or whether you live, is for you to get your heart right with God. You need to know that God loves you, and that He wants you to be happy. You have to make your peace with Him"

But she told me that God was punishing her for her two abortions and for all the bad things she had done. That's how she explained that the cancer had begun in her ovaries. Now they would have to be removed and she could no longer get pregnant. This was God's judgment upon her.

I said, "No. God doesn't work that way. God doesn't give people cancer. You have already asked forgiveness for those things and God no longer holds them against you. You have to forgive yourself as well or you'll never have peace. God loves you and He wants you to be happy."

I went on to tell her that Satan is the creator of cancer, and I quoted John 10:10 for her.

"The thief comes only to kill, and steal and destroy; I have come that they may have life, and have it to the full."

Isn't it ironic that it was just over a decade to this utterance, that I had believed the same terrible things about God? I also had believed that God was responsible for all the heinous acts of Satan and the terrible consequences of sin in our lives. I found myself amazed that God had brought me 180 degrees to the point where I could tell Diana about the true nature of God; that He loves us; that He wants the best for us; that He would never do anything to hurt us. God is our Father, and our Spiritual Father at that. In so many of our lives, our earthly fathers fail us.

Diana's father failed her. My father failed me. But isn't it wonderful that no matter what else may happen to us, we always have a second chance with God? He is our Father, our ultimate Father. And He loves us now and forever more. Never will He leave us - Never will He forsake us. That's a promise that we can always rely on.

Now, as I sit poised over the keyboard, I want nothing more than for Diana to understand the peace and the joy of knowing that God loves her, that He forgives her; that she no longer needs to feel bad about the past. It is all washed away and she has been made clean and new. I want her to know that. I want her children, my children, Cathy and Phillip, to meet her some day in heaven and walk hand in hand and talk and laugh and play. No heartache. No pain. No guilt.

So many divorced men and women take to bitterness, to hating and insulting their former-spouses. I am so glad that I decided to pray for Diana. Yes, it's true; sometimes the only way to keep from hating someone, is to love them. With God's help, I have learned to love Diana. Thank you God for your help. Now help me raise my children.

Diana died on August 24th, 2004, after a long and courageous fight against ovarian cancer.

The last six months of her life, she was the best mother she had ever been. She met God on good terms.

Enjoy the rest of Tim McGraw's lyrics below.

He said "I was finally the husband,
That most the time I wasn't.
An' I became a friend a friend would like to have.

And all of a sudden goin' fishin',
Wasn't such an imposition,
And I went three times that year I lost my Dad.
Well, I finally read the Good Book,
And I took a good long hard look,
At what I'd do if I could do it all again,
And then:

I went sky diving, I went rocky mountain climbing,
I went two point seven seconds on a bull named Fu Man
Chu.
And I loved deeper and I spoke sweeter,
And I gave forgiveness I'd been denying.
An' he said: "Some day, I hope you get the chance,

To live like you were dyin'."

All of us should learn to live like we were dying. Because . . . after all . . . when it comes right down to it . . . we are.

"I've probably eaten some pretty nasty things in my day. Chicken beaks, gums, talons, feathers."

Hot Dogs and Eggs

Yes, even as I write this little story, I'm eating hot dogs and eggs. I've had worse. That reminds me of my time in the Marine Corps. Back in the seventies, they were feeding us all the leftovers from the Vietnam War, which meant mountains and mountains of C-rations. They came in little olive drab tin cans. (That's green to you civilians.) I still have the can opener. We called them John Waynes or sometimes P-38s. I love those little can openers.

Anyways, C-rations were wonderful. Most guys complained about eating them everyday, but I thought they were pretty neat. They had fruit cocktail, crackers, cheese spread, chicken, pork, beef, even spaghetti and meatballs! I think the pound cake actually weighed a pound! Those things could stop an M-16 bullet!

I liked the chicken best, but once I made the mistake of reading the ingredients on the can. It said, "chicken with chicken parts". They didn't mention which parts .

. . just parts. That made me nervous, but I was hungry, so I ate it all, every last "part". I've probably eaten some pretty nasty things in my day. Chicken beaks, gums, talons, feathers. Who says we're not barbarians? Reminds me of McDonalds. "Parts is parts!" Oh well, it's all protein I suppose.

But I think the nastiest thing I ever ate was monkey on a stick in the jungles of Panama. I was at a jungle warfare school for the Marine Corps. It was tough, but I survived. What's that Nietzsche said? "That which does not kill me, makes me stronger." I really don't think Nietzsche would have said that after eating a monkey. It was vile and nasty! I won't even tell you what it tasted like! The Boa Constrictor wasn't bad though. Tasted like chicken. Have you ever noticed that a lot of things taste like chicken? That gets a man to wondering. But I won't go there!

But I suppose that it's the vile and nasty things in life that help us to appreciate the nicer things. Life without extremes would be a very boring place to live. Maybe that's why I like Michigan so much? Without the cold of Winter, I could never fully appreciate the warmth of Spring. And it's the pain of loss that enables me to fully enjoy my friends. Without the full spectrum of good and bad, we are left myopic and bland. Nothing but doldrums on a sea of placid, uneventful calm.

Or, it could be that I have no idea what I'm talking about. You decide.

Well, my hot dogs and eggs are gone now, so I guess I'd better get some work done. Hmm, I wonder if one can still buy C-rations? Chicken with chicken parts? Why does everything taste like chicken? (Except monkey.) I guess that's one of those eternal questions for the ages. We may never know.

Have fun. Now if you'll excuse me, I'm gonna go fry up another hot dog!

"I teach people how and when to kill. I feel good about that."

I Couldn't Kill to

Save My Life

I had a good day. I wrote a chapter to my next novel "*Church and State*", answered email, did some marketing, etc. It was a good morning. Then, at noon, my huntin' buddy came over and we went out for lunch at the local greasy spoon with all the other rednecks. Warm grease makes life easier to swallow sometimes. Not many people know that, so you're lucky I told you.

My friend is a Staff Sergeant with the National Guard and just came home from a year in Iraq. It's good to have him back. I was concerned we'd never get to hunt together again. War changes people. War kills people.

Sometimes I wonder how I'd perform in a life and death struggle. I was 6 years in the Marine Corps, but it was peacetime. I also teach CCW Personal Protection classes, which, at its barest essence means: I teach people how and when to kill. I feel good about that. I know I'm performing a powerful and necessary service to my fellow man by teaching mothers and fathers how to protect themselves and the children they love. I love my job as an NRA Instructor, but I also realize the seriousness surrounding it.

I also know that it takes all kinds of people to make up this crazy world of ours, so I've grown more tolerant and patient with those who don't share my views. After all, I didn't start out perfect either. (Yes, that was a joke.)

I remember several years back I was teaching a class; it was a private lesson with a husband and wife. The mother could not hit the broad side of a barn from the inside. I tried everything I knew to get her on target, but it was no use. I couldn't find the problem. Her husband told me she was a good shot, and that she usually shot better than he did, so he didn't understand the problem either. I questioned her some more, and she finally threw up her hands in frustration and said, "I don't even know why I'm doing this! I could never shoot anyone anyways. My husband made me take this class!"

I interjected. "What if someone was trying to kill you? Could you shoot someone then?"

She said, "No! I couldn't kill someone to save my own life. I'd just go ahead and die!"

I thought that was rather odd, but I could tell she was telling me the truth, so I thought about it a second. Even though most people have an aversion to killing another human, I personally believe that there are very few people who would rather die than protect themselves. Almost everyone has a point where they will cross the line and take a human life.

Earlier in the day, this couple had introduced me to their little girl, so I said,

"How old is your daughter?"

"Nine months."

"Okay, let's use a little training technique called visualization."

She nodded her head impatiently.

"Okay, here's the scenario: You're at the gas station filling your tank. A man drives up and parks next to your car. He gets out, walks over, reaches through the open window of your car, removes your daughter from her car seat and puts her in his own car. He then starts to get into his car to drive away."

There was a horrified look on the young mother's face.

"At that moment in time, could you take another human life?"

Without hesitation she said, "I would kill that son of a bitch!"

I said, "Okay then, that target down there is that man who is stealing your daughter. Fire away."

She never missed the target again.

I think the lesson here is obvious. Sometimes life throws things at us that we don't want. We have to do things we would, under normal circumstances, never,

ever do. Life is full of hard choices.

I'm not advocating that you run out and buy a gun. That wasn't my purpose in writing this. In fact, this little story has nothing to do with guns and everything to do with life.

I am, however, suggesting that you think hard and then make good choices. Because, at the end of the day, we all live or die based on the decisions we make. So make good choices.

> "Patience serves as a protection against
> wrongs as clothes do against cold. For if
> you put on more clothes as the cold increas-
> es, it will have no power to hurt you."
>   --Leonardo da Vinci--

I Feel Like Job

Do you ever feel like the biblical character Job? Job is probably best known for his sufferings, thus the phrase, "He has the patience of Job". Well, I don't have much patience, but there have been times in my life when I felt like Job. I'm 48 now, and the first 45 years or so contained more than my share of pain. An unhappy childhood and two bad marriages brought on a multitude of suffering. But the similarities between myself and Job stop there. Because Job was considered by God to be a righteous man, but no one will ever accuse me of that. Job's pain was precipitated by his righteousness, while mine, was a consequence of my own mistakes.

In retrospect, I shot myself in the foot, not once, but several times. And the thing I kept learning, over and over again, was that every time I shot myself, it caused me pain. It downright hurt. But not only did it hurt me, it also hurt my kids and everyone around me. It pains me to know that my children suffered for my stupidity and my selfishness. I have four children, with one on the way, and my oldest daughter has yet to forgive me for my mistakes. Someday I'm hoping that she does and that our relationship can be healed. But she'll probably have to shoot herself in the foot a few more times. Apparently, the apple didn't fall too far from the tree.

So how am I like Job? With Job, all his riches were restored to him. But I never had riches. My whole life I lived from one paycheck to the next. I believe they call that hand to mouth, for whatever reason. After 40 years of that, a man starts to feel sorry for himself, but self pity is the one thing that he can never afford. It simply feeds and speeds his downward spiral. Not a good thing. But then, I digress.

I feel like Job, because, in the end, I became happier than I've ever been in my whole life. I chose my first two wives based on the weakest part of my character. For most men, the weakest part is just below the waist. But on my third strike, I hit the ball clean out of the park! Sara has made me happier than any person ever could. She has a very strong relationship with God, and she supports me in everything I do. She loves my kids very much and is a true helpmate. Before Sara, just 3 short years ago, I was a single parent, raising four kids, lonely and miserable. I remember on many occasions I used to walk the roads looking for pop cans just to get enough gas money to drive to work the next day. That was an incredibly humiliating experience for me. I hated to walk the main roads for fear people would recognize me and guess what I was doing. But that's where the most money was, so I stuck to the main roads and every time a car drove by, I would turn my face toward the ditch so they couldn't see who I was.

But my life is very different now. I have two published novels with another on the way. I live in the country surrounded by some of the prettiest land you've ever seen. My freezer is full of venison, my truck is full of gas, and I work at home full time writing books and taking care of my family. My dreams have come true.

So what's you're point, Skip? My point is this: Whatever a man soweth, that shall he reap. It took me several years of doing the right thing before my life got better. I had to change and become a better person before I could attract a quality woman like Sara.

All of life is cause and effect: Whatever you sow, you will also reap.

The lesson is this. Sow good seed, and you will reap happiness one hundred fold. Sow seeds of discontent, and you'll harvest a crop of sadness. But you must be patient. It takes time to turn your life around. No matter what happens, keep on trying. Keep on doing the right thing. Have faith in God and great will be your reward,

"'Cause I've got friends in low places
Where the whiskey drowns
And the beer chases my blues away
And I'll be okay
I'm not big on social graces
Think I'll slip on down to the oasis
Oh, I've got friends in low places"
                                        --Garth Brooks--

Friends in Low Places

Ya know a lot of educated people make fun of country & western music, saying it's unsophisticated, redneck, just too simple and too hillbilly. I know I used to look down my nose at it myself. Seems like somebody's dog is always dying or their wife is leaving or they're drinking themselves into a stupor.

I always wondered why anyone would be drawn to that kind of music; it was just too darn negative. I didn't have time for it. And then it hit me about 16 years ago, after my first divorce. I lost my wife, my dog, my kids, my salary, my entire way of life was irrevocably altered forever. I was suddenly thrust deep into the bowels of country & western hell! Finally, I understood.

Buddha says, "All of life is suffering." So does Willie Nelson, Hank Williams, and Garth Brooks. Great minds think alike I suppose. So, perhaps there's more to country & western music than meets the eye. Yeah, sure, some of it is base and primitive and juvenile, but I have to admit; it has a certain appeal. When I was young, it was stupid. Now, it's inspirational and encouraging. What's the difference? What happened to me?

Did I grow up?

Country & western music has a relevance that seems to escape rock-n-roll. It is crux and core and basic to life itself. It deals with the pain of the human heart. I'm reminded of William Faulkner's words:

"The primary job that any writer faces is to tell a story out of human experience – I mean by that, universal, mutual experience, the anguishes and troubles and griefs of the human heart, which is universal, without regard to race, or time or condition. He wants to tell you something which has seemed to him so true, so moving, either comic or tragic, that it's worth preserving."

--William Faulkner—

I recall at age 34 I had never been drunk. I hated the taste of alcohol. It all tasted like cough syrup to me. But then I was divorced and my life was shattered. I missed my children, and I decided to try it. Perhaps it would ease my suffering.

My favorite song quickly became *"Friends in Low Places"* by Garth Brooks.

I remember sitting in a bar one Friday night, all alone, drinking a wine cooler, watching the other people dance, wishing to be held, not knowing how to meet the need, listening to *"Friends in Low Places"*. That experience gave birth to chapter 18 of my second novel *"We Hold These Truths"*. Here's an excerpt that pretty much sums up how I felt.

Hank then turned his attention to the people dancing on the floor. He envied all of them, with their ability to stand in a crowd and block out all else except the music and the feel and flow of their own bodies as they moved across the floor in a feverish act of self-fulfillment. They were oblivious to all else save their own passions and emotions. The waitress walked away.

Hank's parents had never let him dance, had indeed never allowed him to attend a dance during high school, and he would always resent that. Indeed, his feet would not and could not dance, and he felt too old to force them to learn now. But, just for tonight, he was here to watch them, to admire them, to encourage them with his jealousy, and perhaps absorb a bit of their passion and confidence. It was his only way of connecting - his only way of sharing the loneliness. At least he was sharing something with someone.

Caroline had loved to dance, but Hank had been afraid to learn. Perhaps if he had learned to dance, she would not have . . . . He let the sentence die unended. Finally, the waitress came back with his Bourbon, and set it down on the Formica table.

"You don't have to drink the whole thing if you don't want to. I won't charge you for what's left over. Just don't drink out of the bottle."

Hank looked up at her. There were wrinkles around her eyes, the kind not caused by age. Hank tried to smile, but could tell by the look on her face that he'd failed. On a normal day, he would have her laughing in 5 seconds flat. But not today; it just wasn't in him. She walked over to another table, and Hank let her move out of his sight.

I believe that country & western music has tapped into the agony and angst of the human heart, simplifying it, distilling it to its essence. It is the voice and the art of the common man. Perhaps there's more to it than we think.

But I did get drunk on one occasion. I was living in my brother's garage, sleeping on the greasy cement floor, working three jobs, paying more child support than a body has a right to, eating fried squash, wild mulberries, collecting potatoes from the muck fields in Orangeville. On that night, the pain became so great, that I spent every cent I had on a four-pack of Seagram's Peach Wine Coolers. After work, I laid down on the dirty foam pad that I used for a bed, and I watched the Johnny Carson monologue on my little black and white television. After the first bottle, I felt dizzy. The second made it hard to get up. After the third, I could no longer hold my head up. But I have to admit, that Johnny Carson was in great form that evening. Every word he said was funny. I even laughed at the commercial breaks. I remember that my brother walked in after the third wine cooler, looked down at the bottles on the floor and smiled at me. I had been a staunch anti-drinker my whole life, and he was amused at my predicament. After teasing me for a few minutes, he left and I was alone again - alone with my thoughts, my feelings, my pain. - all the things crux and core to life – just the basics - all the things that country & western songs talk about.

Oddly enough, I didn't forget my pain that night. My mind remained as clear as a bell. I just couldn't walk. I blamed God that night, cursing him for my clarity and cognizance, imagining that he was not allowing me to get off so easily. God would not allow me to run from my problems or to drown them in alcohol. Today, I thank Him.

What would have happened to me if the alcohol had worked? I shudder to think of it. And the old saying lingers on: "There, but for the grace of God, go I."

So I thank God that the booze didn't work, that I was unable to anesthetize the pain. I was forced to feel, to think, and to work through it. Isn't it ironic, that my second wife was an alcoholic? I suppose that means something. I'll have to drink about . . . I mean, "think" about that for a while. It would appear that God's plan for my life doesn't include alcohol or any other "easy" way out.

So, as I sit here in my car, typing away on my laptop, nursing a 16.9 fluid ounce bottle of Mountain Dew, I thank God that the alcohol didn't work, and I was spared that vice.

And all the Southern prophets, Willie, Hank, and Garth, all join in with a resounding "Amen!

Bottoms up, and have a great day! "

"Remember that one camping trip where it rained all week and you got that awful rash on your butt?"

I Like Rocking Chairs

I'm sitting in a wooden rocker, with my back slider door open, listening to the small creek that runs through our back yard. It's not really a creek, but we like to think that it is. It's more of a seasonal washout that fills with water every time it rains, mostly in the Fall and Spring. It's a cold day for mid-May, but I don't mind the breeze coming into the house, so long as the sounds and smells come with it. I can always put on a jacket.

The rocking chair is my excuse to slow down and enjoy life, like they did on Walton's Mountain way back during the depression era. Those were hard times I suppose. I don't know firsthand. I wasn't born until the late fifties, but my parents and grandparents always talked about it, with its harshness, it trials, its challenges. But the odd thing about it, was that they always seemed to have a twinkle in their eyes and a fondness in their voices whenever they spoke of hard times. I didn't understand that when I was a kid, but now that I have more miles on me, I think I do.

I think it's like the family camping trip from hell. You know what I mean; the one where it rains all weekend and everyone is stuck inside a small tent, fighting, squabbling, eating cold food, no showers, everyone grumpy with frayed nerves and big frowns. The kids keep saying "When is it going to stop raining?" Then on the way home, the car breaks down and you spend two days, and money you don't have, waiting in a far-off town garage for parts to come in from East Cupcake, Montana.

Finally, you get home and everyone relaxes. But the weird thing is this: a year or two goes by and everyone in the family starts to laugh about the camping trip from hell. They make jokes about it. They say things like: "Remember that one camping trip where it rained all week and you got that awful rash on your butt?" The kids like it, despite the fact that they complained and screamed bloody murder while it was happening. Eventually, it becomes part of the family history, part of the folklore told around Thanksgiving dinner tables 30 and 40 years into the future.

The two older kids are in school right now, and Cedar is sleeping in the car seat, so it's just me, sitting here in the rocker, typing on this laptop, listening to the rain fall on the roof, the water rushing down the creek, and the wind blowing in and chilling my bones. But I don't care.

I'm happy. It's a joyous contentment. I'm remembering the time just last week when Cathy and Phillip jumped into a giant mud puddle they optimistically refer to as "the pond" and came out looking like giant pollywogs. It took hours to clean their clothes and get the mud out of their shoes, but that distasteful memory is already fading. All I can remember now is their screams of delight and the splashes as they jumped into the mud, over and over and over again.

And I think that's what they'll remember a half a century from now in their rocking chair days as well. They'll think, "Wow! Do you remember that giant lake we had in our back yard and how we used to swim in it all the time when it rained." Of course, it wasn't a giant lake, just a big mud puddle. But that won't matter to them, because the puddle will have served its purpose. The puddle sparked their imaginations, brought them closer together, brother and sister, bonding, laughing, crying, talking, living life together as only family can do.

> "All our knowledge merely helps us to die a more painful death than animals that know nothing."
>
> --Maurice Maeterlinck--

My First Cat Autopsy

I just finished my first cat autopsy. I never thought I'd have to do that. Phillip, Cathy and I got a big surprise this morning when we went outside to leave for school. There lay their beloved pet cat, Chia, in front of the truck, deader than a doornail. Phillip started wailing immediately and ran into the house. Cathy just cried quietly. Personally, I never liked that cat. (Does that make me a suspect?) I only tolerated it because I love my kids and they loved him. It took them 15 minutes to calm down, then I got them to school late.

After a thorough, post-mortem examination, I have determined that the cat was mauled to death by our beagle, Sherice. I never liked that dog. The right, back leg was broken. I surmise that the cat froze to death over the night. I won't tell the kids that their dog killed their cat; that would only complicate matters, and, since I'm not a licensed forensic pet doctor, I can't be positive about the cause of death. As far as I'm concerned, the cat was run over by a car and limped up into the yard to die of internal injuries. Hopefully, God won't send me to hell for something like that. I doubt he will. He has bigger fish to fry than me.

So, I've prepared the body for burial, wrapped it in towels, and covered it with cinnamon, nutmeg and vanilla. (I was fresh out of gold, Frankincense and myrrh.) Some of my redneck friends may be confused at this point: "Are ya gonna eat it, or bury it?"

Rest assured, the cat is prepared for internment behind our house in a newly established pet cemetery. I made the casket from a cardboard box and duct tape. For all my liberal friends, relax, the cat and the casket are all fully biodegradable. The cat should decompose and quickly return to that "great circle of life". There will be no viewing, we had that this morning in the front yard, and the funeral service will be held promptly at 7PM tonight. Friends and family of Chia are all welcome. Kool Aid, graham crackers, and ice cream will be served immediately following the service.

I've never prepared a cat for burial before, so I hope I'm doing this correctly. When I was a kid, we always just threw them in a hole out back or gave them to the pigs. Pigs will eat anything.

I suppose to say that I hate cats is a strong statement. I've had many cats in life, none of which I've loved, but

I recall one point in my life where God sent a cat to answer a prayer of mine. I don't remember the cat's name or eventually what became of it, but I recall everything else about him. He was dark grey, with short hair, dark eyes, and rather aloof. The cat didn't like me, and I didn't like him. Typically, we went out of our way to avoid each other.

At that point in my life, I was in the initial death throes of my first marriage. My wife and I were seeing a marriage counselor, but nothing seemed to help our relationship improve. I remember how I felt though: sad, miserable, and all alone. That was a few years before my first son was born, and the meaning of life had not yet been revealed to me. I was a wreck.

We lived in downtown Grand Rapids, in the old part of town, the Heritage Hill District, in the top half of a duplex apartment. It's odd, but I even remember the street address: 842 Lyon NE. Isn't it interesting how we can remember the most mundane details decades later, but are unable to recall where we put our car keys a half hour ago?

I was lying on the waterbed in our bedroom, all alone in the house. It was quiet, except for the sound of my own crying. I remember explicitly what I told God at that dark night of my life. I said, "God, I'm lonely. Please hold me." A few seconds later, the cat hopped up on the bed and brushed itself against me. I pushed it away, but it came back and lay on top of my chest and purred. I took my forearm away from my eyes and looked into the cat's face. He licked me, and I knew at that moment that God had not forsaken me.

Life is full of unusual surprises. My ailing marriage was to limp on for about 6 years after that, but even though I wasn't going to church, I still felt like God was with me, that He would never leave. He was there for the asking.

God has always been like that. To Him, a promise made is a promise kept. I wish we could all be like that. I will always remember that cat and that one time he held me. After that, we went back to avoiding each other. But the one time was good enough. It reminded me, once again, that God is there, in all things, even the simple things, and He loves us and never will forsake us.

It's a promise we can take to the bank: "Never will I leave you. Never will I forsake you."

Blending a family is tough enough, but try blending 5 kids from three different mothers and getting them to live in peace and harmony under one roof. Here are my oldest two, Chris and Marissa, at the hospital when Cathy was born. By the time this picture had been taken, they had already finished sibling class and were happy to have another child in the house.

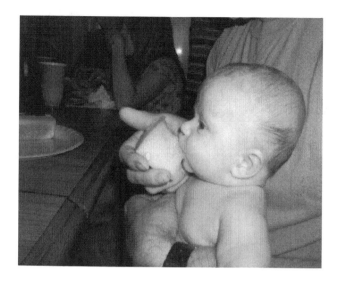

"Love at first bite!" We discovered at 4 months old that Cedar loves watermelon, so when he started teething, we froze it and let him suck on it to relieve the pain in his gums.

My oldest son, Chris, is now 20 and works on staff with Youth With a Mission in Wisconsin. He's a little scruffy now, but still as cute as the dickens! Cathy and Phillip miss him very much.

My two oldest, Chris and Marissa, play with baby Phillip on the floor. Babies always bring the family closer together, if you do it right.

Here is my great, great grandfather Clarence, my great, great grandmother Naomi, and the little boy is my great grandfather Earl. The Coryell family came to America in the 18th century and settled in New Jersey and later in Pennsylvania.

This is my grandfather, Jerome Edward Coryell Sr. He lied about his age and enlisted so that he could fight in France during World War I. Not many people lie about their age in order to fight for their country, but it was more common back then. My legal name is Jerome Edward Coryell III, so I feel a bond between my grandfather and my father.

This is my mother and father on their wedding day on November 5th, 1954. Mom gave birth to seven children: Connie, Jerome (Skip), Debra, John, Charity, Glen, and Alicia.

My daughter Cathy and her friend Doey. Cathy found this big White Morel all by herself on our property. See chapter titled "A Fungus Among Us" to read more about fungus and family. I convinced my children that I could smell the mushrooms when they got close, and then I would guide them to the right spot. My kids and I have enjoyed hunting for morels every Spring. Fungus is a family thing at our home.

This is Sara's mother and father. They live in Newport, Oregon. I owe them a debt of gratitude for raising up a godly woman. It hardly seems fair; they did all the work, and I reap all the benefits!

On July 3rd, 2004, Pastor and friend, Jeff Arnett, united us in holy matrimony at beautiful Bowens Mills Historical Village in Yankee Springs. Sara looked beautiful. But I was just a redneck from Orangeville. It's amazing that after 5 kids and three wives I still have my hair. I suspect that I'm growing old from the inside out. One day soon I'll wake up bald and wrinkled. Won't Sara be surprised? (Photo courtesy of Bowens Mills Studio. www.bowensmills.com)

> "Keep away from people who try to belittle your ambitions. Small people always do that, but the really great make you feel that you, too, can become great."
>
> --Mark Twain--

My White Feather Dream

One of my favorite books of all time is called "*The Dream Giver*". It is an allegory similar to "*Pilgrim's Progress*" and was written by a man named Bruce Wilkinson. In the book, the main character is named *Ordinary*, and one day Ordinary finds a white feather lying on the ground. (Throughout the book, white feathers are symbolic for each man and woman's personal dream. In the story, God creates every person for a special purpose, and he gives them each a feather. It is the choice of the dreamer either to take up their feather and make the dream come true, or to leave it lie until the window of opportunity is gone.) Ordinary picks up the feather and decides to make his dream come true, but, before he can do that, he must first leave his home town called

Familiar. (Does any of this sound "Familiar"?)

At first, Ordinary is afraid, but more and more, with each passing day, Ordinary becomes unhappy with his dull, monotonous life and he decides to leave Familiar. Besides, the white feather of his dreams, given to him by God, is burning in his heart. But the most unexpected thing happened to Ordinary on the way to making his dream come true. Many of the other people in Familiar resisted his departure; when Ordinary followed his dream, it made the other people of Familiar feel uncomfortable.

In the end, there were many obstacles that Ordinary had to overcome before making his dream come true. In the end it happened, but not until life had knocked him down a few times and beat the stuffings out of him. But Ordinary kept getting up and moving on, taking the white feather of his dreams with him. Finally, God asked Ordinary to dedicate the dream to him, and he did so and was used by God in a great way.

But despite the happy ending for Ordinary, there's just no getting around it: making your dream come true is not an easy thing, and it makes some people feel very uncomfortable.

Today, as I write, I can't help but feel like my life has gotten seriously, perhaps irretrievably off track. Of course it's just a feeling, and, like most feelings, it will be gone in a few minutes or hours or days and tomorrow I'll be my hopeful self again. But let's face it, life is rough, and sometimes I get down in the dumps and my hopes become skewed and waning. I lose sight of my white feather and start to feel like my dream will never come true.

Even in retrospect, I'm not quite sure how I fall into these dark moods. Sometimes I can feel the icy grip of despair closing around my throat and dragging me under for the third time. That mood is coming on me now, and, no matter how hard I fight, it continues to drag me down. Birthdays do this to me. They make me think and re-evaluate my life.

In a few months, I'll be a half century old. You'd think a man this lived would have more answers, but I just don't. I can remember small glimpses of my child-hood: feelings, smells, isolated events that took place. But things are getting blurry now, and I just can't stop the memories from fading away. I suppose some of that is a good thing. Does any man really want to remember everything that ever happened to him? "Not I said the cat!" Life isn't that good. I'll just grow old gracefully and welcome senility according to God's divine sched-ule.

Looking back, I can remember the eager hopefulness of my twenties, how I could run for miles without stop-ping, how I could lift, and bend and carry and stretch; then wake up the next morning without a pain to show for it. Now simply waking up is synonymous with pain and stiffness and carries the same angst as a 20-mile marathon.

I still recall my thirties, though the memories are fast fading. Somewhere among those years I slowed down. Perhaps it was the extra ten pounds that held me back? I was no longer young, but not yet middle aged. The great things I was supposed to accomplish were still undone, still just plans, still hopes, unrealized, unsung, undone. But there was still time, still time. Still . . . no . . . time did not stand still.

And my forties came upon me like a storm, like a black wind in the night. And those dreams are still undone, still just hopes in my head, bouncing around like ping pong balls over uneven rock and I can't catch them. Every time I think I have one, it takes a bad bounce and off it goes. But I chase after it, like the wind, always unsteady, always unsure, always hoping.

And then I realize that there comes a time in a man's life when he has to re-evaluate, he has to scale back his dreams, he has to be reasonable and settle for something between himself and the stars. Is that time now?

I'm 49 years old, but. . . I'm just too stubborn. I don't want to give up. I won't give up. I won't stop running and chasing after my dreams, no matter how much it hurts in the morning. I'll take the pain as it comes as payment for the honor of chasing my dream for just one more day. To be honest, there are some mornings when I would like to give up, would, indeed, relish the thought and the . . . . . No. I can't think that way. I can't give in to it. I have to keep fighting, keep working, keep moving forward, keep believing, keep dreaming. Yes, keep believing in the dream, my dream. Don't let it die.

Yes, I just need more faith, and faith is the only thing that can move mountains. Keep working, keep making it happen, one tiny little speck at a time. I can move a million grains of sand. I just need time. Yes, I can move the mountain. It just takes time. Do I have enough time? Only God knows. Hmmm, makes me wish I'd started sooner. Guess I'd better work faster.

Never give up. Hold on to the white feather of your dream. Because, when you surrender your dream, you die.

"I have spread my dreams under your feet; Tread softly because you tread on my dreams."

--William Butler Yeats--

My dream of being a writer has come true! I feel like John Boy Walton with adrenaline! (And a baby.)

My Dream Come True!

Well, I've been working at home full time for a few weeks now, and I have to say that I really enjoy it. I find myself working 12 hours a day but never feeling mentally tired. It's not what I thought it would be. For years I've fantasized about this dream, and my fantasy looked something like this:

6AM - Wake up.
7AM – Wake up again.
8AM – Wake up, think. Go back to sleep.
9AM – Wake up. I'm hungry. Get out of bed. Eat.
10AM – Answer all my fan mail.
11AM – Think about writing something.
Noon – Eat lunch.
1PM – Think about writing something again.
2PM – Write something.
2:30PM – Exhausted. Take a nap
4PM – Grant audience to Producers, Agents, Editors and other assorted important people, all seeking to benefit from my fame and talent.
5PM – Choose one sycophant and allow them to buy me dinner.

7PM – Check my email again.

8PM – Watch television in an attempt to find that elusive inspiration.

Midnight – After a long, hard day at work, go to bed, exhausted and fulfilled.

Here's how my day really looks:

6AM - Wake up. Check email.

6:30 AM –Get my wife off to work.

7AM – Wake up the kids and get them off to school.

8AM – Sit in front of my computer, behind my particleboard desk in my canvas folding chair and try to think of ways to get people to buy my books.

9AM – Eat a bowl of oatmeal. Send out emails to promote my book.

10AM to 10:05AM – Answer all my fan mail.

10:05AM – Do the dishes.

11AM – Work on promoting my books.

Noon – Eat lunch.

1PM – Update my website. Do laundry.

2PM – Write something.

2:45PM – Get the kids from school.

3PM – Do homework with the kids, play hide and seek, convince children to leave me alone so I can write.

4PM – Write.

4:30PM – Make dinner.

6PM – Greet wife at door. Thank her for supporting me while I make my dream of writing come true. Promise to make us rich someday.

6:30PM – Eat dinner with family.

7PM – Try to convince my wife and children to let me write. (Wife says, "You've been home all day, what have you been doing?") I smile and promise to do better tomorrow.

7:30PM – Give up on writing and watch reruns of "*The Waltons*" with my family.

8:30PM – Get the kids ready for bed.

9:00PM – Tuck kids into bed.
9:30PM – Check email. Plan for the next day of work.
10PM - After a long, hard day at work, go to bed.
2AM – Wake up in a cold sweat, after having a nightmare about writer's block and lack of time to write. Lay awake until 5AM.

Yes, I am exaggerating. It's fun though, isn't it? My wife and kids are all very supportive, and I do get enough time to write during the day. But I've noticed that it's much easier to write a novel than it is to sell one. For every hour I write, I must spend 5 hours trying to market it.

I'm just no good at self-promotion. It makes me feel vain.

But this is my dream, so I work hard, doing whatever it takes to make that dream come true.

So I guess I'm a stay-at-home Dad/Writer. But I like that too. In fact, my wife will be having a baby in March. Stay tuned to see what my schedule looks like then. No problem – plenty of time to sleep after I die.

Well, gotta go pick the kids up from school now and get dinner started.

Make it a great day!

But the one constant through all of life is the river. It is permanence in motion. It feels no guilt at its lazy ways. It just keeps on flowing, regardless of what foolish men may think about it.

Permanence in Motion

I'm sitting here in my new home in Eastern Iowa, watching the ice on the river float on by. It's 11AM and everyone else in the world is at the office, or the factory, or the store. They're all out in public, punching a time clock, following checklists, taking orders, filling orders, lifting things, loading things. But I'm sitting here in the living room, looking out my window at the Wapsipinicon River and it's beautiful. I've been working full time at home as a writer for the past year, and I have to admit that I'm still trying to figure it all out. The problem is – I feel lazy. No matter how much I write, how hard I edit, how diligently I market, I can't help but feel a twinge of guilt at my situation. After all, how many of us get the opportunity to do what we love? Not many. I know that to be true from experience, because for 25 years I worked at a job I hated. Most of us do that. We work to eat, or eat to work, and sometimes the two blend together so much we get confused.

But the one constant through all of life is the river. It is permanence in motion. It feels no guilt at its lazy ways. It just keeps on flowing, regardless of what foolish men may think about it. Over the past year, I've had to re-evaluate my definition of work. Even as I write these words, I don't feel like I'm working; it just feels good to get it out, to be true to myself, to do what God created me to do. And if . . . if people can glean some better understanding of themselves, of humanity, and of life by what I write, then . . . perhaps, just perhaps, I've done my job. And hasn't that always been the job of the writer, the artist, to help everyday people remember the important things in life? I certainly think so.

So, in that regard, I am working very hard. When I take a walk in the woods – I am working. When I sit in the kitchen looking out the back window while sipping hot cocoa – I am working. When I gaze out my front window at the Wapsipinicon river, watching the January ice flow down stream, when I let my mind wander and slow down, when I give myself over to God's time and just think and ponder the greatness of everything around me, that's when I do my best work.

And, I suppose, only a writer can get away with doing things like that. After thinking about it some more, I guess I should feel guilty. But, somehow, I'll reach down inside myself and find the inner strength to carry on. In the meantime, I'll just finish my hot cocoa and watch the river. After all, it's my job; it's what I do.

So go ahead and relax a little bit today and just think about the river, learn from it and enjoy it. I think that's one of the reasons God made it. Relax and enjoy - permanence in motion.

This chapter is dedicated to Henry and Ethel McClure of Kansas. You are both fine examples of this country's greatest generation. Thank you for your service.

Henry and Ethel McClure from the heartland of Kansas. (Sara's grandparents) They exemplify our greatest national treasure.

Old People

At 7:55 a.m. Hawaii time, a Japanese dive bomber bearing the red symbol of the Rising Sun of Japan on its wings appeared out of the clouds above the island of Oahu. A swarm of 360 Japanese warplanes followed, descending on the U.S. naval base at Pearl Harbor in a ferocious assault.

It is Pearl Harbor Day, and there's a lot on my mind – lots of problems, personal things, things that seek to destroy those I hold dear. Despite that, I have to take a moment to reflect on the blood and sacrifice of our fathers and grandfathers. I love spending time with old people – they are the crux and core of our society – the glue that holds our culture together. And I shudder to think what will happen when these human, national treasures are all gone.

My grandmother was one of the greatest influences on my young life. She taught me to cook from scratch; she led me to Jesus; she told me about the depression, growing up in the muck fields, and the Second World War. She's dead now, and I shudder to think what will happen when all the old people are gone. Old people are the heart and soul of our nation; the conscience of America; the disappearing link of common sense and logic.

What will happen when they're gone? What will become of us and our children?

Who will pass on our history and humanity to the next generation?

I don't know.

But I maintain that there is hope. America will prevail. Humanity will prevail.

I believe that the world doesn't exist for the individual, but the individual exists for the world. To find the meaning in life, you must first find something greater than yourself to serve. Through service to others, life is given meaning.

Now is the day to decide: "Who is my master? Who shall I serve?"

Because everyone serves something, either knowingly or unwittingly.

There is a hierarchy to all of life; there is a master; there is a servant. The happiest people in life, the ones we remember and revere, and respect; they are the ones who have selflessly served; they are the ones who have sacrificed. And the greater the sacrifice, the greater the remembrance.

Jesus once said:

"If you want to be great in God's kingdom, then first,

you must become the servant of all."

I quote Jesus a lot, not just because he is the son of God, or because of his powers or his miracles, but because of his sacrifice. Jesus also said, "Greater love hath no man than to lay down his life for his friends."

And that is the ultimate sacrifice isn't it? To die for another person? Many of us would die for the ones we love, but Jesus went further than that. He died for the unlovable. He died for murderers, rapists, thieves, and the selfish of this world. And then he commanded us to be like him. That seems like a tough act to follow.

Perhaps that's why I look up to old people so much. There is a term in theology called "sanctification" which means, "the process of becoming more like Christ". Old people are better at this, because, well, they're old. They've been at it longer than the rest of us, and sanctification is a lifelong process. There is no "self" in sanctification, only Christ, the master, the author, the finisher of our faith. The old people I look up to and respect have figured that out, and they practice it.

I remember when my grandmother died. She was a pillar of the community, and loved by all. Her funeral was a very happy time. She lived in the country, but hundreds of people came from all around, people whose lives she had touched in a positive way. Towards the end of the funeral service, people were given the opportunity to come up and say something about her. Many came up, and all had the same message. She never thought of herself. She sacrificed. She gave to others.

My grandmother was the wife of an alcoholic, whom she served, loved, and tolerated for 30 years until he died. But, despite her suffering, I never felt sorry for her. I don't think anyone did. She suffered quietly, through her pain, and she focused on the things she had control over – herself and her actions. My grandmother had a great attitude, and it was infectious. She spent her life striving to become more like Jesus, and, because of that, others in turn, tried to become more like her.

Early in my life, I respected her and tried to be like her. Later in life, I caught a glimpse of the person she was looking to off in the distance, and I moved my eyes toward Him. In the end, I did become more like her. She introduced me to her master, and I chose to serve him too. I have never regretted that decision.

And now, my children look to me, and I can't help but wonder. What do they see? Who do they see? Do they see Skip, the flawed man, the selfish one, or do they catch a tiny glimpse of the man I'm looking off to in the distance. I hope and pray it is the latter.

I believe that old people are the backbone that hold us up and keep us moving in the right direction. I shudder to think of it, but it is likely that someday you and I will be old people. The mantle of responsibility will fall to us. We will take over where our parents and grandparents left off. Will we do a good job? Who will people see when they look at us? Will they see Jesus, or will they see the flawed, selfish one?

I don't know. I can only hope and do my best.

Viola Coryell, my grandmother, was one
of the greatest influences of my youth.
She taught me to cook from scratch;
she led me to Jesus; she told me about
the depression, growing up in the muck
fields, and the Second World War.

"You can never escape who you are, no matter how far you roam. You can run, but you can't hide from your childhood. The past latches on to your coat-tails and you drag it, kicking and screaming into the future. "

Norman Rockwell

with a Hangover

I grew up in this tiny, little Michigan town, called Orangeville; it was barely a whisper on the map. We had a general store across from the gas station, and a small tavern across from that. Oddly enough, we had four churches, but I think the tavern did the better business despite the fact it was outnumbered four to one. Much of the clientele was the same, and I'm sure many of the congregations met at the tavern to discuss the sermon on Sunday afternoons. I find it strange that I grew up in that town, and still live nearby, and though I've attended all four churches, I've never set foot inside the tavern.

Am I better than other people? Anyone who knows me can answer that without hesitation. "No!" I just didn't go in there, because I didn't want to get beat up. The place had a reputation I suppose, and well earned. I remember once, as a child, I peeked inside the door, but only for a second. I didn't want to be corrupted, so I didn't dare linger. But I don't want to talk about drinking today. I think I just mentioned it, because I want to write about my roots.

My hometown was a mixture of light and dark, shadow and sun, good and bad; and I think if anyone were to paint a picture of it, they would have to name it *"Norman Rockwell with a Hangover"*. Kind of like a Mad magazine version of *"The Waltons"*. Everything looks okay on the outside, but dig a little deeper and you discover that: John Boy has a porn addiction and writes articles for Playboy; his father, though he tries to make ends meet, has to subsidize the family income by cooking meth in the old abandoned barn on the back 40; and Grandpa Walton, the family patriarch, has been banging the Baldwin sisters for decades.

Yes, okay, so I'm exaggerating. It wasn't that bad. In fact, I love the place and I miss my childhood for a host of reasons. After high school, I moved off to college and didn't make it back for 20 years. But the whole time I was off living in the big city, my heart never left that little town. In my first two novels *"Bond of Unseen Blood"* and *"We Hold these Truths"* there is a character who has left town, only to return to his or her roots for comfort. You can never escape who you are, no matter how far you roam. You can run, but you can't hide from your childhood. The past latches on to your coat-tails and you drag it, kicking and screaming into the future. But I wouldn't have it any other way. I wouldn't give up my dysfunctional childhood for all the money in the world. It made me who I am, and I have learned to like myself.

In "*We Hold These Truths*" Angela Benning returns to Freidham Ridge after the attack on nine-eleven. She needs the security and familiarity of her home town. She just can't get that old theme song from "*Cheers*" out of her head.

> *"You wanna go where people know, your*
> *troubles are all the same. You wanna go*
> *where everybody knows your name."*

I really enjoyed that old sitcom with Sam and Norm and Woody and Cliff. I feel safe when I sing that song. I moved back to the country about 2 years ago and never regretted it. I like the smell of my wood fire and everything else that it represents. Nothing but neon in the city, and I have no use for it. I left the rat race, and I haven't looked back.

But whether your roots are in the city or in the country, one thing rings clear: ya gotta have roots, or you flounder through life. I've seen people like that, and I feel for them. They are the restless souls who've never lived in one place more than a year at a time, always moving from town to town, job to job, school to school: known by many, befriended by few, residents of the world, but citizens of nowhere. I feel for them; they are always visiting, but never home.

I may be just a weed of a man, but I have roots, running deep and strong, never failing, always there, rock, steady, and sure. It reminds of a country & western song by the group "*Alabama*":

> *"I was born country, and that's what I'll always be,*
> *like the rivers and the woodlands wild and free.*
> *I got a hundred years of down home,*
> *runnin' through my blood.*
> *I was born country, and this country's what I love."*

Life is full of pain and suffering. In fact, Buddha taught, that all of life is suffering. But I don't cotton much to that, and I'm certainly not smart enough to argue with Buddha. But I do know that much of life is pain, and, that without God and our families, most of us wouldn't make it through life as well as we do. God and family make the pain in our lives bearable. It's where we turn when the bottom falls out. All of us, when we get into trouble, we return to our roots, to God and to our families.

Isn't it a shame that sometimes we wait so long?

Signing off for now, but hoping you have a place to go down home where everybody knows your name. Make it a great day!

> "When I was a child, I spoke as a child, I understood as a child, I thought as a child: but when I became a man, I put away childish things."
>
> --I Corinthians 13:11--

Playing with Toys

This morning I was speaking to my 11-year-old son, Phillip. He was eating his cereal before school and I was just standing there at the counter watching him. Suddenly, quite out of place, I said, "Ya know, Phillip, you are going to have a wonderful life. You're going to be a great man when you grow up. You'll have a good job, and you'll do good things."

He just looked at me blankly and said. "Okay."

I went on to say, "And you're going to marry a wonderful woman and have kids for me to play with."

My young son laughed and said, "Dad, you're crazy. I don't like girls."

Have you ever noticed that children can seldom see beyond the toy they're currently playing with? I wonder if that's a bad thing? And I wonder if adults are really a whole lot different? I think not.

I suppose we're good at staying focused, perhaps even obsessed, but far-sighted? I don't think so. I think only a wise person can see beyond his actions to the subsequent consequence or reward. Most of us just play with our toys, whether that means fishing, or work, or TV, or whatever.

Then, we get to the end of our lives and realize that we played so much for so long that nothing is left but a long trail of broken toys that no longer excite us. Like children, we viewed life with little or no hindsight, thus, the toys we chose were but fleeting, unimportant objects that didn't stand the test of time.

Don't get me wrong. It's good to play - even necessary to a degree - but all mindless play with no thought to the future leads to an old man in a rocking chair, contemplating the long list of regrets that make up his life.

That reminds me of a verse in the Bible:

I Corinthians 13:11

"When I was a child, I spoke as a child, I understood as a child, I thought as a child: but when I became a man, I put away childish things."

I'm not so sure that's true anymore. It seems to me that people, men especially, are maturing much later in life, or not at all. We see men in their forties still living at home with their mothers, being waited on hand and foot.

I recall a movie last year titled "*Failure to Launch*"

that dealt with just such a phenomenon. Their son, Tripp, played by Matthew McConaughey, is 35 years old and still sleeps upstairs on a twin bed with Superman sheets he's had since he was six years old. In his own words, "It's going to take a stick of dynamite to get me out of my parent's house. " Eventually, his parents, played by Kathy Bates and Terry Bradshaw, hire a professional motivator who promises to get him out by simulating a romance. In the end, Tripp fell in love and moved out of the nest, but, in real life, more and more, men are refusing to grow up and are staying home with momma.

Not to sound cold, but, when my kids graduate from high school, they're off to college or the military. Anything different is dealing them a disservice, and I love them too much not to kick them out of my house.

So, to that end, I strive now, while he's still a child, to teach Phillip all the things he needs to know to become a man. Self reliance, hard work, honesty, ambition, and kindness to others. And, hopefully, by time he hits 18, he will voluntarily put away childish things and become a productive member of society.

And, when he marries one of your daughters, he'll open the door for them, speak kindly, work hard to support them, be a good father, and make those around him feel happy and safe.

So, do me a favor, raise your kids the same way, so that my son has a host of good women to choose from. But there's no hurry. After all, he's only eleven.

Jesus, my friend and hero, revealed himself to the riff-raff and rabble of the world as well as to the rich and powerful. He partied with the IRS; lived with fish mongers; ate with noblemen; and drank with everyone.

Rednecks and Rich Folk

Sara would get upset at me for being in here with the baby. I'm in a smoke-filled greasy spoon, ordering sausage, eggs, and orange juice. Everyone else is chain smoking and talking about Nascar, the weather, even using profanity, just for fun I think. What is the big deal with profanity? I've never understood that. Why do people curse? For effect? In my writing, I use it sparingly, and try to come up with creative ways to avoid it. The guy at the table next to me, wearing an olive drab, military field jacket, toting a weather-hardened face, greasy hair and laughing eyes that have seen better days, just told a redneck joke in hushed tones, as if it was something he'd get in trouble for. I wonder if he realizes that he's a redneck too?

The waitress just brought up my order and said, "There ya go honey!" She can't be more than 18 years old, and already she's calling a 48-year-old man, "honey". There are words on her t-shirt that read: "I may not be perfect, but there are parts of me that are pretty awesome!" I won't ask her which parts. Besides, according to McDonald's, "parts are parts".

In my novels, I love to create characters with low, social standing: the poor, the frail, the feeble minded, all those who are considered by society as substandard, and I like to elevate them, and use them as vehicles to dispense wisdom to the rich and powerful of this Earth. I love the riff-raff and rabble of our nation, because, of course, "I are one".

The Bible talks about money, more than any other subject. I recall the verse which says: "It is easier for a camel to pass through the eye of a needle, than for a rich man to enter the kingdom of heaven." I used to wonder what Jesus was talking about, but now I think I understand. It's not just about greed, money and riches; it's also about power and pride. After all, isn't pride one of the seven deadly sins? I understand the lure of pride firsthand. People need to feel good about themselves, but sometimes they make the mistake of lowering others to raise themselves. I've done this many times myself, and I usually end up going back and apologizing to people I've wronged. In the end, a man searching after God will often find humility somewhere along the way.

And I guess that is why God judges people by the content of their heart and not by what they wear, or eat, or drink, or how long their hair is, or how many body piercings they have. None of us have a corner on heaven or on righteousness. We will all answer to God as equals.

I'm reminded of a scene in the movie "*Robin Hood: Prince of Thieves*" with Kevin Costner, where Robin Hood (Costner) and the Maid Marion are speaking. Robin and Marion, deep within the secure bowels of haunted Sherwood Forest, are speaking of nobility and the common man.

Maid Marion says, "How is it that a once arrogant, young nobleman, has found contentment living rough with the salt of the earth?"

Robin's reply is profound truth, spoken with the wisdom of a warrior, who has lived through the pain and suffering of many battles.

"I've seen knights in armor panic at the first hint of battle. And I've seen the lowliest, unarmed squire pull a sword from his own body to defend a dying horse. Nobility is not a birthright, it is defined by one's actions."

Sometimes I feel sorry for people like the ones here at this greasy spoon. Many of them are of lowly birth, disadvantaged in life, simply by their own lineage and genetics. But at other times, I envy them. They work hard, with little or no prospect of bettering themselves, but they work hard nonetheless. They love their children, they go to church, they vote, they pray, and buying lottery tickets seems their only hope of ever making the American dream come true. But they do all this with a clear conscience, and they sleep well at night. In that sense, they are all knights in shining armor.

I'm suddenly reminded of a scene from "*It's a Wonderful Life*" with Jimmy Stuart and Lionel Barrymore. In the scene, Henry F. Potter (Barrymore) is badmouthing the common folk of Bedford Falls, and George Bailey (Jimmy Stuart) defends them in a vehement and angry voice.

"Just remember this, Mr. Potter! That this rabble you're talking about. They do most of the working and paying and living and dying in this community. Well, is it too much to have them work and pay and live and die in a couple of decent rooms and a bath? Well, my father didn't think so. People were human beings to him, but to you a warped, frustrated old man, they're cattle. Well, in my book he died a much richer man than you'll ever be."

Jesus, my friend and hero, revealed himself to the riff-raff and rabble of the world as well as to the rich and powerful. He partied with the IRS; lived with fish mongers; ate with noblemen; and drank with everyone. He was the hero and savior to redneck and rich folk alike. I think if Jesus were here today, he'd like Nascar as well as the opera, and that's no small feat. He'd probably go to the ballet, drink a glass of champagne, eat those fancy, little finger foods, then, afterwards, go to the pub, and watch a big screen TV with the rednecks. On Sunday, he'd go to church, then afterwards, attend a barbecue, turn water into Bud Light and enjoy roadkill on a grill.

After reading through this a couple of times, I've come to realize that there's not much difference between the rich and the poor, save their possessions. But, in the end, we can take nothing with us that we have not already given away. We are all laid to rest in much the same fashion. We live – we die – the dirt is thrown on our lifeless face and we return to the dust from whence we came.

The rich and the poor, the king and the peasant, the master and the slave; in the end, we all die and stand naked before God. In death, we are all the same. So should it be in life. God loves us all, and in His eyes, we are nobles.

"Miles to go before we sleep . . . and miles to go before we sleep."

--Robert Frost--

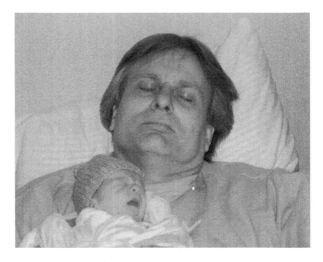

Cedar Lance Coryell. Baby number 5. They'll find me in the morning, a pulsing mass of protoplasm, slowly soaking into the carpet. Dead by morning. Forty eight years old and still popping out puppies.

Post-partum Puke-n-Poop

On March 1st, 2006, my wife, Sara, gave birth to our son: Cedar Lance Coryell. It has been 9 years since I've dealt with babies. They have a way of taking control. They are, simply put, "Carpe Diem" incarnate. How can 5 pounds, 7 ounces of baby, dominate the destiny of an entire family with a combined weight of over 500 pounds? I don't know, but I'm starting to remember.

No sleep.
Eyes drooping, bloodshot, in pain.
Newborn baby crying, in my arms.
Awake all night, pooping with a vengeance.
Can't type with one hand.
Baby cries – I jump.
Going crazy without sleep.
Need a break. Won't get one.
Gotta do work. Gotta write. Can't write.
2AM, all hope is lost.

They'll find me in the morning, a pulsing mass of protoplasm, slowly soaking into the carpet. Sleep. Need sleep. Can't sleep. Dead by morning.

I'm 48 years old! What have I done?

Baby cries – I jump. Diapers cascade around me.

Stinking convergence. Wet wipes are my only friend.

Puke-n-poop all around me.

Two voices, one weak, one strong, battle it out inside me for dominance.

The weak voice says.

"But I remember the sleepless nights and I don't like it!"

The strong voice counters.

"Don't worry. There's plenty of time to sleep after you die."

"But I remember the diapers and I shudder!"

"No, it's like riding a bike. You just change them. Out with the old and in with the new!"

"Oh no, why did I do this? I'm going to die!"

"Relax, we all die someday."

"But this is child number five."

"In biblical times, children were a blessing from God."

"I knew better than this."

"There's a baby in the crib that says you didn't."

"Most of my friends are grandparents and I'm still

popping out puppies!"

"Yes, and isn't he cute!"

The weak side of me pauses, looks into the crib and smiles.

"Skip, get hold of yourself. You've done it before. You can do it again."

"Yes, he is cute, isn't he. Maybe I can do this one more time."

I pick up the baby and rock him gently in my arms. He is wide awake at 2AM, but very cute. Did he just smile?

Finally, he sleeps.

I'm awake. I look at him, so peaceful, so vulnerable, so needing.

I provide. I protect. He needs me.

My son. I love him.

Plenty of time to sleep after I die.

"I guess it's not so bad. I suppose I can do it one more time."

Slowly, I fall asleep. My little son barely opens one eye, looks up at me, and smiles.

"Come on Dad! You can do it! Just one more time! I'm counting on you!"

> *"Miles to go before we sleep . . . and miles*
> *to go before we sleep."*

I reach down to my side and lovingly
touch the grip of the .40 caliber pistol
for reassurance. Is .40 caliber enough?

Rodents of Unusual Size

I killed another ROUS last night. They seem to be
taking over the entire house. They live underneath, and
then come up through the ductwork at night. They are
very large, and seem to be getting bolder by the day. I've
killed three so far in the last two days, and I just heard
two more running through the heat ducts a few minutes
ago. They don't scamper like other animals of their kind,
they seem to gallop or trot. I find it very disconcerting,
especially at night.

But Sara and I have taken it all in stride and try to
look at the positive side. Why just this morning I told
Sara, "Look on the bright side, they scare away the
mice." Scare them, or eat them, I'm not sure which. But
the nagging question in my mind remains: "What happens when they outgrow the heating ducts?" What will
become of my family? Will we be overrun? Will my

military prowess be enough to save the day? These are all questions, nagging at the inside of my brain. Where is Bert Gummer when you need him?

I've cleaned my guns and bought extra ammo. What more can I do? Note to self: "Need to buy a pair of Night Vision Goggles." These animals are cruel, heartless devils, hell-bent on destroying my family!

Damn! There goes another one! They make the floor vibrate when they run! I reach down to my side and lovingly touch the grip of the .40 caliber pistol for reassurance. Is .40 caliber enough? Should I buy another high capacity magazine?

Last night Sara and I huddled together in bed, afraid for the children, wondering, "Is tonight the night?" I put out a box of food laced with poison. They left a note: "Thanks for the veggies, but we need red meat!"

What would Ted Nugent do? Probably turn the house into a giant speaker system and explode their brains with rock-n-roll. Note to self: "Call Ted's Manager. Schedule a one-time gig."

Perhaps I was too quick to blame our beagle for the death of our cat. Our other cat ran away three days ago. Reminds me of the old saying: "The cats are abandoning the ship."

But don't worry about us. I didn't spend 6 years in the Marine Corps to be driven off by a herd of ROUS's. (Rodents of Unusual Size) Now, if you'll excuse me, I'm off to my workshop. I'm trying to build a better ROUS trap.

Lord, make my aim straight, and my heart pure and true.

(ROUS - supplemental)

I just killed another one. The fiends are getting smarter! I had to chase this one around the room with a hammer before I was able to subdue him. I tried to make him talk, but he just smiled, and gave me the finger. I gave him the hammer. The filthy, black-hearted beast!

Rest assured, with God as my strength and my witness. Good will overcome.

Captain's Log – ROUS Body Count

Captain's log, star date 19 January 2006. All rodents of unusual size have been destroyed and peace has been restored to the galaxy. The final body count was 6 ROUS's, confirmed dead. Their bodies were disposed of without pomp and ceremony in the woods behind my house.

Question: Did their lives have meaning and purpose? Or, did they simply exist? Will the snuffing of their lives affect the greater life force that is and does and breathes all around us?

Do I care?

Nah! They're just rats. I killed 'em all!

"Why would God give me an insatiable desire for something and then tell me not to do it? I incorrectly reasoned that God must be cruel. So I turned my back on him. I thought I could do it better without Him."

Sergeant Johnson

Sex is everywhere! Billboards, television, radio, the movies, the office, magazines, you name it. There is no escaping sex. It is everywhere. Why is it so important? I've often wondered about that. I read somewhere that men think about sex several hundred times per day. I can't verify that, since I've never bothered to count. But I know it must be a lot, else it wouldn't give rise to such a huge industry worldwide.

I used to think about sex a lot more when I was younger, but not as much now. I always hated the fixation and would struggle to think about other things, but it was primarily a losing battle. In my younger days, especially my twenties, I think I could actually feel the hormones physically coursing through my veins, taking control, raging within, threatening to override any rational thought. It was almost like I had two heads: the big head on top of my shoulders, and the little head, down below my waist. Being in the Marine Corps, I sometimes took a military approach to my life. I gave the little head a name: Sergeant Johnson. And every morning, Sergeant Johnson would wake up and snap to attention, give me that big, one-eyed salute and say, "Good morning sir, permission to take the helm?"

And most days I would wisely say, "At ease, Sergeant. Stand down." But my character wasn't always that good, and my second marriage was at least partly attributed to Sergeant Johnson and his exploits.

After my first divorce, I remember losing all hope and faith in God. I had viewed marriage as the bedrock foundation of society, something permanent, immutable, something that would last forever and stand the test of time. After all, people just didn't get divorced when I was a kid growing up in the country. It truly was "till death do us part", even if one spouse had to kill the other.

But after that first divorce, I was never really the same. In some ways, I became better, eventually, but in others, I became worse, by giving up my childlike faith in God. It is a sad thing to lose one's foundational beliefs. Without knowing what I was doing, I made a crucial mistake that altered my life forever, causing pain to all I touched.

In my mind, I thought: "All my life, I've strived to

obey God's commands." I waited until marriage at 23 years of age to have sex, and that was a big sacrifice for me, since most of my peers seemed to be doing it. (It was the seventies.) Then, during ten years of marriage, my wife and I had sex less than ten times. We never did make love. Nonetheless, I stayed loyal to her. I never strayed. When it came to sex, I had more fidelity than RCA Victor. But then, after 10 years of sadness and misery, she divorced me. It didn't seem fair. I blamed God.

I reasoned that the things I was taught as a child must be wrong, because they didn't work for me. Why would God give me an insatiable desire for something and then tell me not to do it? I incorrectly reasoned that God must be cruel. So I turned my back on him. I thought I could do it better without Him. That was an incredible revelation for me which totally revolutionized my life. If God is cruel, then He's the bad guy. I don't have to listen to Him. There are no moral absolutes, and I can pick and choose as I please. What a freeing thought. Within a year of my first divorce, I became "sexually active".

Don't misunderstand me, deep down inside, I knew I was wrong. I just didn't care. I was mad, and a small measure of anger could justify a multitude of sins, at least in my mind. I dated a beautiful blonde woman for the next three months. The sex was great. Then she dumped me, leaving me more heartbroken than before. On the heels of the biggest rejection and heartbreak of my life, came another, and I was left worse off than before. I rebounded with my soon-to-be second wife, who turned out to be addicted to drugs and alcohol. I knew I had no business dating her, let alone marrying her. But Sergeant Johnson was calling the shots, and I had given him full control. He was my god now.

My girlfriend became pregnant. Have you ever noticed how people who want to downplay their actions, speak and write in the passive voice? Somehow, mysteriously, she "became" pregnant. Let me try that again. I got my girlfriend pregnant. I put a bun in her oven. I knocked her up. I played park the porpoise one too many times, and I got caught. Did I love her? No. I was using her, and she was using me. Later on, I grew to love her, but it was not so in the beginning.

I thought I knew better than God, and I screwed up. That one, selfish act, has probably caused more pain than any other thing I've done. It started off a cause-and-effect chain reaction that continues to this day. The consequences of some mistakes stick with you for a lifetime.

I thought I knew more than the architect of life. God made me. He designed me. He knows all our tolerances, what is good for us and what is bad for us. He knows what we can handle and what we can't. Why? Because He designed us and made us. God truly knows us inside and out. God invented sex. He understands that sex is a spiritual act that merges two people's souls. That's why He reserved it for the stability and permanence of marriage. He is our Father. He loves us. He wants to protect us from the soul-wrenching pain that unmarried sex inevitably brings. I understand now.

So why did He have to make it so darn fun and irresistible? Good question. I can't fully answer that. I'm not the creator. I am the created.

But I think, that maybe, God has a purpose in everything. Solomon said, "There is a time and a purpose for everything under the heaven." I guess that must include sex as well. I believe that God's purpose for sex was twofold: it gave us a fun way to procreate, and it brings husbands and wives closer together by merging our spirits.

Everything has a purpose; every tool has a proper use. Proper use brings reward, while misuse brings consequence. That is the natural order of things, the way it's supposed to be. I learned that the hard way. And my purpose in telling you this story, is so that you can learn from my mistake, thereby, avoiding all the pain this mistake caused me.

God used that mistake and its accompanying pain, to teach me and to make me a better person. Now I have more to offer Him, via the people around me.

Yes, Sergeant Johnson has a time and a purpose. But, no matter how he may beg, whimper, moan and plead to be let out to play, don't let him. He's a little beast that will ruin your life and the ones you hold dear. If you have to, bust him down to Private Johnson until his appointed time.

Trusting God will save you a multitude of pain. Listen

131

to the architect of creation. Read the specification and follow the user's manual. You won't be disappointed.

"When there is no time for being there is no time for listening. I will never understand the silent dying of the green pie-apple tree if I do not slow down and listen to what the spirit is telling me, telling me of the death of trees, the death of planets, of people, and what all these deaths mean in the light of love of the Creator who brought them all into being; and you."

--Madeleine L'Engle--

There is a Rhythm

There is a rhythm developing in my life, and I like it. I have slowed down, not from age or from temporary circumstance, but from thoughtful, well laid-out plans, which are finally taking root and giving fruit. Every morning I awaken at 6AM with my wife. She does her exercises while I try to find my pulse. Around 6:15, I manage to fall out of bed and land in the shower. Once the water hits me, I'm alive again, vital signs resume, and my day begins. I get Sara off to work, then the kids off to school. By then the baby is ready for his morning nap, and I am free to write - free to think, to create, to co-create with Christ.

A few minutes ago I was sitting in the truck with the

window rolled down, listening to the birds and smelling the Spring air. I didn't sit there because I had to, or because someone paid me to do it. I did it because I wanted to, because my soul yearned for the doing. And because I obeyed the natural longing of my soul, I now feel relaxed, rejuvenated, and refreshed. All is well.

But I remember a time, not too long ago, when the rhythm of my life was nothing short of dissonance and confusion, a sad mixture of running too fast, for too long, with too little to show for my efforts. It reminds me of that Jackson Brown song: *"Running on Empty"*. After 20 years in the corporate world, I noticed a pattern. Men and women would work for 30 to 40 years, then retire. We would give them a party and send them off on their new life of relaxation and comfort, where they would do all the things they had been waiting their whole lives to do. A few years later, sometimes just a few months, I would read their obituary on the company bulletin board. Inevitably, someone would always comment, "Didn't they just retire?"

I don't want that to happen to me. I have a lot more living to do in whatever time God has allotted me. I don't want to waste it.

I recall a very odd couple from my childhood. They lived just a quarter mile down the road from our house. Jenny was a college librarian, and Cal was an engineer. They had no children, just two incomes and lots of stuff. I think back then we called them yuppies. I'd never seen a yuppie before. But they were nice people and I liked them.

I always looked on them with awe, because they had so much money. We were poor, so they got my attention when they drove by pulling their large sailboat to Lake Michigan. They were my idols, and I wanted all that money too.

But then something really weird happened. All of a sudden, they both just up and quit their jobs. It was the strangest thing. They started walking around in bib overalls, chewing on grass, moving real slow and just making things they had a mind to.

I remember that in my teenage years, I spent a lot of time down there, mostly doing leatherwork, birdwatching, candlemaking, and watching Jenny make quilts. Most weekends Cal and Jenny would travel around the state to arts and crafts festivals peddling their wares. Sometimes I would go with them, and I really enjoyed it. But I came to understand very quickly that there was very little money in art, so I shied away from it. I didn't want to be poor like my parents.

Now, 35 years later, I live much the same way that Cal and Jenny did (minus the bib overalls) and I've come to understand and appreciate their decision to leave the rat race behind. In the end, I had to make the same tough decision. I could have kept my corporate job, making a decent wage, buying lots of stuff, living in a big house with two new cars, but, in the end, I decided against the "decent" wage, in lieu of a "decent" life. Of course, either decision would have been okay for me to make, but only one would have made me truly happy.

And that's the big decision we all have to make. What will make us happy? We have to figure out what that wonderful and elusive "something" is, and then we have to go for it, or not.

But whatever you decide, I hope and pray you are happy, that you somehow tap into God's perfect rhythm, that you hear the birds, smell the grass, and feel the breeze on your cheek.

It's almost time for the baby to awaken now, and when he does, I'm going to take him into the woods. Together, we'll watch the shadows drift down through the trees, feel the sun on our faces, and hopefully, we'll find out what kind of birds are making all that noise. And Cedar and I will sing along with them.

Photo courtesy of Phillip Coryell

"I wasted time, and now doth time waste
me."
--William Shakespeare --

The Coin of Your Life

I'm going to take time to relax today, because I need it. I just finished reading through a bunch of internet wisdom quotes on the subject of time, and I realized that no one else knows what they're talking about either. There is nothing new under the sun, and we just keep on learning and relearning, saying and resaying, all the old things from time immemorial. There is nothing I can say that is new; nothing I can write that hasn't been written before. Actually, now that I think about it, isn't what I just wrote from the book of Ecclesiastes? Let me look that up a moment.

Yup, there it is. Just as sure as I'm Walter Cronkite. Ecclesiastes 1:9

"What has been, will be again: what has been done, will be done again; there is nothing new under the sun."

Amazing. So why do we even bother? Why does God even let us go on? It's been over ten thousand years and we still haven't gotten it right. We just keep doing the same things over and over and over again. Vanity, vanity, all is vanity. (That sounds familiar. I'm a shameless eclectic.)

Whoa! I feel a mid-life funk coming on. Oh the agony! The despair! The wretched puke and putrescence that makes up our lives. Oh shut up Skip! You're giving your brain a headache. I'm starting to sound like someone who stays home all day with too much "time" on his hands.

There is never enough time – never has been – never will be. It reminds me of that movie with Bill Murray, "*What About Bob?*". Neurotic patient, Bob Wiley, is having a serious discussion with Sigmund, the 12-year-old son of Dr. Leo Marvin (played by Richard Dreyfus). Sigmund is pretty screwed up too.

"Bob? Are you afraid of death?"

"Yeah."

"Me too. And there's no way out of it. You're going to die. I'm going to die. It's going to happen. What difference does it make if it's tomorrow or in 80 years. Much sooner in your case. Do you know how fast time goes? I was like 6 yesterday."

Bob replies.

"Me too."

Sigmund is getting distraught now at thoughts of his impending death.

"I'm going to die! You are going to die! What else is there to be afraid of?"

Now that's a good question: "What else is there to be afraid of?"

A lot of us Christians say: "I'm not afraid of death." In fact, there's a verse in the Bible that says; "To live is Christ, to die is gain." I think a lot of us Christians are lying. We are afraid.

It's one thing to say you're not afraid, but it's really quite another to live like you're not afraid. If a man sticks a gun in your face, are you afraid? I think my pulse would quicken. I am afraid of death. But I think there's something that I'm even more afraid of: "I am afraid of life."

So, in an effort to make every second count, I become incredibly efficient. I use time management software programs. I write out a to-do list everyday. I prioritize the tasks. I cram as much as I can into every second of everyday. The world looks on and says, "Wow! He's a hard worker. He gets things done. He's got it all together."

But at what price? Sometimes my stomach hurts. I can't sleep. I get headaches.

"Time is the coin of your life. It is the only

coin you have, and only you can deter-

mine how it will be spent. Be careful lest

you let other people spend it for you."

--Carl Sandburg--

In the movie, "*Lord of the Rings – The Fellowship of the Ring*", deep in the mines of Moria, Frodo and Gandalf speak privately:

Frodo says in frustration.

"I wish the ring had never come to me! I wish none of this had happened!"

Gandalf replies in a fatherly and sympathetic tone.

"So do all men who live to see such times. But that is not for them to decide. All we have to decide, is what to do with the time that is given to us."

So today, as in every day, you and I must decide what to do with the time that is given to us.

Will we waste it? Will it waste us? Will we use it? Will we spend it wisely? And who decides what is wise and what is foolish? And why am I wasting my time trying to figure it out when so many wiser men before me have failed?

I don't' know. But I think it's in my nature. It's pathological. Men cannot stop asking unanswerable questions. It's deep in the race. God made us this way.

Perhaps a better question might be: "What am `I' going to do today?"

Will I make the world better? Will I play with my

kids? Will I be kind to my wife? Will I treat God with reverence and respect? Will I stop, just for a single moment, a tiny, single second in time, to watch in awe and wonder, the creation of God, and worship Him for it?

I don't know? I'm just a man. But I'm going to email my wife and tell her I love her. Then I'll make dinner for the kids. Then, if there's enough "time", I'll go check the mailbox outside. And, while I'm walking in the cold, I'll appreciate how warm it is inside my house. And I'll pause for a moment, long enough to watch a tiny snowflake drift lazily down through the winter sky.

What will you do?

"What the caterpillar calls the end of the world, the master calls a butterfly."
                                        --Richard Bach--

Tuna Fish on

White Bread

This is a brand new year, and all I can think about is tuna fish sandwiches on white bread, with mayonnaise. My wife tells me that white bread isn't good for me, but I like it anyways. I grew up in the shadow of the cold war, with the ever-present threat of nuclear annihilation, reading books like "*Alas Babylon*" by Pat Frank, wondering what I would do if I survived a limited nuclear strike. Compared to all-out nuclear war, white bread seems like a small enough threat.

As a child, some nights I would stand outside, look to the north, and see the lights of Grand Rapids reflecting off the clouds 35 miles away. Then I would look to the south, and see the white haze of the lights of Kalamazoo off in the distance. I grew up with my fingers crossed, hoping that those two cities would be spared in a war. I suppose that's why I blew up Grand Rapids in my second novel, *"We Hold These Truths"*. I just didn't want the threat hanging over my head anymore.

It seems that there will always be some kind of grave threat hanging over our heads, suspended there, threatening and ominous. In my father's childhood, it was the Nazis and Japanese; in mine, it was the Cold War; and now, for my own children, it's radical Islam and the War on Terror. Jesus said that the poor will always be with us. I suspect that war is the same way. I'd like to believe in peace on earth and good will toward men, but I just don't see it happening.

It's a confusing thing to spend one's childhood looking over your shoulder, waiting for the bright orange ball, exploding in the sky. Thank God it never came. But if it had, I can't help but think, that tuna fish sandwiches on white bread, with mayonnaise, would have been lost forever. The thought makes me shiver.

Have a bright and happy new year!

> "The unexamined life is not worth living. "
>   --Socrates--

Untasted Orange Juice

Beside me is a TV tray, and resting on it is a glass of orange juice. This orange juice is special. It may be the last orange juice I ever taste in life.

I am sitting in my Lazy Boy recliner, with my laptop on a pillow. The back side of the laptop is propped up by a hardcover book on electrical engineering; not because I love engineering, but because it is the proper thickness to reduce glare on my computer screen. Life is full of orange juice, so much so, that we seldom pause to taste it. Today, it is the untasted orange juice for which I mourn.

My wife and I have an agreement, and it works for us. I will stay home and write, clean the house, take care of the kids, while, she, in return, will go to work everyday and pay the bills. I suppose it is an unusual arrangement, one that few would consider, but it is a happy arrangement for both of us.

This arrangement allows me to think; it allows me to ponder; it allows me to reflect. Life has become so busy, that I suspect not much of that goes on anymore. There is no time to think; no opportunity to ponder; perhaps even no more desire to reflect. And that is why I write these books. I am a hired pen, a penslinger, so to speak. I think and write, so that others can go about their lives at the speed of light, and, every so often, they can open this book and reflect on the simple, human, universal things of life. It is a sad state of affairs, this human condition.

My orange juice is gone now, but I purposefully drank it slowly, reflecting on the taste, feeling the tiny bits of pulp against my tongue, letting the liquid linger, just a moment, allowing me to glean every ounce of satisfaction. This orange traveled a great distance to reach me up here in the north country, and I appreciate it with an unflinching resolve.

I suspect that millions of people, drink millions of ounces of orange juice every morning in America. Their orange juice is much like mine, with one, very important difference: at this moment in time, I fully understand that this could be the last orange juice I ever taste. I don't say that to be maudlin or overdramatic. I really mean it.

Lately, my 11-year old daughter has become terrified that I will die. Every night, I pray for her, hug her, then tuck her in for the night. As I'm leaving, she always sits up in bed, reaches out her arms and says, "One more hug Daddy, in case I don't see you again."

My little girl understands what most adults do not. We are only visiting this planet, and life is so short and tenuous, and it goes by us so quickly. Each time you hug your child may be the last. Your next breath, your next heartbeat, your next thought – may be your last. I guess that puts a little different spin on life doesn't it?

We are here, but for a moment. Our lives are tiny whispers, crying out, struggling to find meaning and purpose. My life is a subtle vapor; it rises up in the morning, is caught on the wind, then comes the sun – and it is gone.

Please remember this when you kiss your wife good bye, when your children ask you to play, when your neighbor needs to talk, and when a friend needs a favor. In the grand scheme of things, your life is but a tiny vapor. But even a tiny vapor has the power to hurt or to soothe.

And suddenly, I have a craving for another glass of orange juice. And this one, quite possibly, could be my last.

Make it a great day! (It could be your, . . . well, you know, last.)

"You can turn painful situations around through laughter. If you can find humor in anything -- even poverty -- you can survive it."

--Bill Cosby--

Watering Down the Milk

My wife does the bills, because I'm no good at it. Anything money, belongs to her. Last night she came to me and said, "Skip, we need to cut back on our expenses. We're not doing so good." I said "Okay. I've been there before." So, this morning, I cooked French toast for myself and the kids. It wasn't very expensive; nothing but white bread, eggs, and milk. (I threw in a little nutmeg and cinnamon for flavoring.) When I started to put the milk back into the refrigerator, a thought occurred to me. "We're going to run out of milk if I don't do something." So I went to the sink, turned on the cold water and filled the jug back up. Crisis averted. Thanks to quick thinking by Skip's Brain, that was the cheapest milk we ever bought. It's only 8AM and I've already earned my keep. It will be interesting to see if anyone notices the water in the milk. I doubt they will. I can't see through it yet.

I suppose I should be worried about our finances, but I'm not going to. I happen to know that my wife will worry about it enough for both of us, so any added effort on my part would be redundancy. Besides, quite frankly, I've never had it this good. Whenever things get really bad, I can always look back on my childhood for comfort. That's one of the benefits of growing up poor. I remember one time my parents brought home a giant trash bag full of bread and pastry from the bakery. It was filled with cinnamon rolls, pies, and my personal favorite, raisin bread. We ate until we got sick, and then mom put the rest in the freezer.

It never bothered me that the bread had gotten so old the bakery wasn't allowed to sell it anymore for human consumption. The outlet store just bagged it all up and sold it for pig food at one dollar a trash bag. We had a few pigs, but the bread never made it out to them. Staleness never tasted so good!

One of the things I remember most about my mother, was that she would home can just about anything that stopped moving: green beans, waxed beans, corn, creamed corn, beets, meatballs, spaghetti sauce, mince meat, jams, jellies, even ketchup. Most of it tasted pretty good. However, some of it, well . . . sorry Mom, thumbs down on the home-made ketchup. I never did like that stuff. But the rest was great!

My mom did pretty good with money and finances.

My dad, on the other hand, he couldn't hold onto a penny if it was lodged deep inside his colon. He should have just given mom the money, but he didn't. He was always taking out loans, always spending tomorrow's money today. I learned a valuable lesson from my dad. Give mom the money. Thanks dad.

My father was a bit eccentric. Okay, a lot eccentric. He was a child during the great depression, and I don't think he ever noticed that it ended. Back in 1974 when all my friends were smoking dope, having unbridled, irresponsible sex and dropping acid, we were still milking our own cows, churning our own butter, and making our own cheese. (Author's note: the cheese was terrible. It squeaked when you chewed it and felt like rubber.) Even now, I can remember thinking, "Dad, why are we doing all this? They sell butter and milk at the store. Why do I have to get up at 6AM every morning to take care of these stupid animals? I may have even verbalized my concerns – one time. My father was very proud of his self sufficiency, and he was going to maintain it even if it took every dime the family had. And it did.

I used to think my father was so stupid, and I never really understood him. Then I married Sara, animal lover extraordinaire, Sara, queen of the humane society. That woman is a zookeeper in an engineer's body. I spent all last week building a goat pen and a chicken coop. I hate chickens. I hate goats. They are the bane of the world.

Last night we got seven hens and one rooster. I'm

going to kill the rooster. He won't stop crowing, and he deserves to die. I sat down and figured out the money we'll be saving from the eggs they produce. After building supplies, feed, straw, and special egg laying mash, we'll be saving a grand total of $ -7.13, every week. That's assuming of course that all 7 hens lay one egg every day. No problem, if they don't produce, the hens will die. Can you say "Finger lickin' good?" Of course that begs the question: "What are we going to do with 49 eggs every week?" Just thinking about it sends my cholesterol skyrocketing.

All you animal lovers out there are going berserk right now. "Oh my God! He's going to murder the chickens." Hey! Relax! Colonel Sanders made a living at it. Besides, my wife would never let me kill the chickens. I can hear my wife now, desperately trying to reason with me. "But Skip, it's the atmosphere we're paying for, not the eggs." I respond as best I can half asleep. "Honey, it's 4AM and the rooster needs a wristwatch. This isn't ambience, we're living in poultry hell!"

But with the goat, I see potential. I may never have to mow the lawn again! And that's something to crow about. Well, I'm out of time to write now. I have to go feed and water the chickens. Now where did I put that shotgun?

"Government is like a baby. An alimentary canal with a big appetite at one end and no sense of responsibility at the other."
                                    --Ronald Reagan--

We the Sheeple

I was out fishing today, just sitting there, watching my line delve down into the depths of the water, looking at the swans across the way, listening to the woodpecker off in the distance, and feeling the gentle rocking of the boat on the water, and it suddenly occurred to me, "Skip, you're different than most people."

I was just reflecting on my life, all I've said and done, all the many things that have happened to me, and I had to admit: I am a different man than most people. Not better, not worse, just different. Some would say, even strange.

How am I different? I'm not sure. I just know that people look at my life, or listen to me tell about it, and they get this horrified look in their eyes. I just seem to take my life for granted, and it didn't hit me until I asked myself this question: "What would you think about someone you met who was just like you?"

Case in point, I was in Sunday School class this morning, and I heard a man say: "I've had five kids from three different wives, and I'm 48 years old and still having babies when most of my friends are becoming grandparents."

And the most terrifying part was - the man's voice was my own.

I didn't quite know what to think about that. Am I crazy? Am I nuts? Nope. Just different.

I've made a lot of mistakes; that's for sure and I would be a fool to deny it. There are many things I've done that I would be loath to do again, and many things that have happened to me that I wouldn't wish on my enemies. But one thing is for certain, I've always tried to keep a good attitude, no matter what the situation, and I've always tried to accentuate the positive. In keeping with that personal survival policy, I've become very adept at converting manure into fertilizer.

I suppose there's no intrinsic harm in being different. I know I certainly enjoy it. But I've noticed over the years that there's a price to pay for nonconformance. Up until a few years ago, I lived in the city, where conformity is treasured and perhaps even worshipped.

But I don't conform. I'm different.

I remember how much I used to loath city life, and I remember how much the city loathed me. They had this silly thing called the municipal code, which seemed designed to make everyone look the same. The municipal code was a very caring document, and it took a detailed interest in everyone's life, telling them how to act, how to dress, and how to talk. The code took a special interest in people's houses and yards, mandating, under penalty of fines and potential jail time, that the grass in your yard not be taller than 9 inches. I suppose I took issue with that. It was my yard, and, therefore, none of their business how tall the grass was. I've always believed that the length of a man's grass should be dictated by the climate and prevailing weather patterns, not some silly man-made code.

I've always been confused as to why people allow themselves to be overgoverned. We elect leaders, who appoint bureaucrats, who run our government, who run our lives. These people invade our privacy and tell us how to live, and we pay them to do it. And anyone who disobeys, (i.e., doesn't conform) is seen as riff-raff and rabble.

I grew up in a land far, far away, called "the country", and if one neighbor had a problem, he walked over and said, "Hey Zeke! I got a problem with your grass. It's too long." Then Zeke would say, "Hey Frank. If you think my grass is too long, then get your butt over here and mow it. You have my blessing."

Problem solved.

But that doesn't work in the city, because people are

afraid of each other. In fact, many won't even talk to one another. That's why cities have such large police forces. If the people have a complaint about their neighbor, they call 911. Then the police come and say, "We've received a complaint about your dog barking too loud, and if he doesn't quiet down, we're going to give you a ticket and take some of your money."

I used to get letters from the city all the time. "Clean this up!" "Cut down that tree." Mow your grass!" After a few years it became very predictable. So I just decided I wouldn't do anything until the government told me to do it. That worked much better for me. Why, I remember one particular summer it hardly rained at all and I only had to mow my yard two times. I discovered that if you waited long enough, the mowed grass clippings were so thick, they would deny sunlight to the lawn below and kill the grass. Problem solved.

But what is it with conformity? Why is it important enough to send someone to jail over the length of their grass? I never understood that. I think it must have something to do with security, because, in my experience, security is the only human need strong enough to get people to give up their freedom.

What was it Benjamin Franklin said, "Those who would give up essential liberty to purchase a little temporary safety deserve neither liberty nor safety." Not bad for an old, dead, white guy.

Am I blowing this out of proportion? Maybe.

Maybe not. I guess it depends on how far the city goes. Sometimes I wonder, are we people, or are we sheep? Perhaps neither. Maybe we're evolving into a whole new species called "sheeple".

Think about it.

> "My illness is due to my doctor's insistence that I drink milk, a whitish fluid they force down helpless babies."
>
> --W.C. Fields--

Duct Tape, Diapers, and

Yellow Cottage Cheese

Sometimes I wax eloquent – other times – I just wax. I was looking through some of the incredibly profound and relevant issues I've been writing about lately, and it just seems to me I need to lighten up a bit and take a break. Sometimes I think too much, and I don't want that. I could end up with an aneurysm or some such thing, and that sounds painful to me.

So tonight, I think I'd like to talk about bowel movements. And not just any old bowel movement, I want to talk about baby bowel movements. Take my new son for instance. That boy makes me proud every time he grunts for glee. There's a rare conviction in everything the boy does, whether he screams, cries, eats, or just plain poops. A person should take pride in his work, and baby Cedar can grunt with the best of them. He screws his face up into a serious frown, wrinkling his countenance to the core, and then he releases with a jolt that could only be measured on the Richter scale. Thank god the stuff isn't radioactive.

And have you ever noticed the pretty colors? Breast milk babies seem to be pooping out nothing but yellow cottage cheese. It's the weirdest thing I ever saw. Ah yes, the sights and sounds of babyhood. The squirting, the grunting, the screaming, the streaming, the gushing, the geysering. For any normal person, all that would lay a man to waste. But for my little son, it's all in a day's work. Yup, he's doin' the two-step puke-n-poop.

And every time that boy fills his drawers, yours truly changes the diapers. I've given up counting. Suffice it to say I can change that diaper in less time than it takes a champion cowboy to hogtie a calf. And there are some similarities I might add. His little, skinny legs get to kicking and I have to hold him down just to get the job done. Let it never be said that I can't take out the trash. Duct tape, don't leave home without it.

So it's with a great sense of honor and pride that I write of my son and his bowel movement bonanza. That boy is a champion, a baby above men, the stuff of legend. So now, as I turn my ear to his farting in the distance, and feel the earth shake beneath my feet, I sigh, grab the baby wipes, and move in for the spill. After all, it's my job. I'm the Dad. He's my boy!

Come on son! Let it rip! Make me proud!

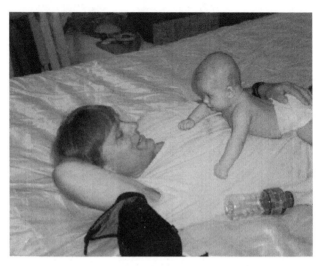

There's nothing like a newborn baby to give life
meaning, to inspire new hope, and to remind an aging
man what is most important in life.
(Now if I can just get some sleep.)

In Closing

Well, okay, so that's about all I have inside my brain
right now. I've probably raised more questions than I've
answered, but life is like that I suppose.

But that one, nagging, resilient question remains:
What is the purpose of life? I don't know for sure. I'm
not so arrogant as to claim that supreme knowledge. But
this one thing I do know. Without faith in God, without the bond and support of family, we will never have
the courage to seek out the higher questions and find the
meaning of life. Faith is choosing to believe in something we can't see. In that regard, all of life is faith. We

believe in air, though we cannot see it. We suck it in and taste it and breathe it, and in return, it gives us life to live another day, another hour, another minute. Without faith we are dead.

Either we believe and seek to find the meaning of life, or we disbelieve and give in to despair. To ask the right questions, to share life with the ones you love, to raise a family, to reach out and sacrifice yourself for the benefit of those you love, to reach out, to touch . . . I don't know if that is the sole meaning of life, but I do know that it gives life meaning.

Yes, without faith we are dead, and without family, we have no reason to live.

May God bless you and your family.

Skip Coryell - 2007

I'm 52 year's old and still popping out puppies.
(Well, okay, my wife does all the hard parts, but I was
there, every step of the way!) This is our newest son,
6-month-old Phoenix Quinn Coryell.

Author's Update

I wrote the majority of this book back in 2006 and
2007 during a transitional time in my life. I had just quit
my long-time corporate job and started working at home.
Since then we've moved to Iowa for a year and then back
to Michigan again. Sara just had another baby last year
and is already talking about another. Baby Phoenix is
cute and lots of fun, but I'm not sure how I feel about
another one. Then again, I've never been much good
at telling my wife no, especially when saying yes is so
much fun!

On the professional front, I've started my own business called White Feather Press, and it is going very well. Initially, I was just going to publish my own writing, but things have snowballed out of control and I now have a dozen authors. It's lots of fun and I'm meeting some really good people and publishing excellent writing. You can check them all out at www.whitefeatherpress.com.

In the meantime, stay close to God, Family and Country and you'll never go wrong.

God bless you all and thanks for reading my work.

Skip Coryell - 2010

About the Author

Skip Coryell now lives with his wife and children in Michigan as a professional writer, and "*Laughter and Tears*" is his seventh published book. He is an avid hunter and sportsman who loves the outdoors. Skip is also a former Marine, and a graduate of Cornerstone University.

For more details on Skip Coryell, or to contact him personally, go to his website at www.skipcoryell.com. (email: skipcoryell@hotmail.com)

All Skip Coryell's books are available for purchase on www.whitefeatherpress.com. You can read all about Skip Coryell, his life and his work at www.skipcoryell.com.

Novels

Bond of Unseen Blood

We Hold These Truths

Church and State

Stalking Natalie

Nonfiction

Blood in the Streets

RKBA

Laughter and Tears

Made in the USA
Charleston, SC
10 April 2015